TOMMY SMITH
AT THE ZOO

Books by
Edmund Selous

Tommy Smith's Animals

Tommy Smith's Other Animals

Tommy Smith's Birds

Tommy Smith at the Zoo

Tommy Smith Again at the Zoo

The Zoo Conversation Book

*The Zoo Conversation Book,
Hughie's Second Visit*

Jack's Insects

TOMMY SMITH
AT THE ZOO

by

Edmund Selous

with illustrations

YESTERDAY'S CLASSICS

ITHACA, NEW YORK

This edition, first published in 2018 by Yesterday's Classics, an imprint of Yesterday's Classics, LLC, is an unabridged republication of the text originally published by Methuen & Co. Ltd. in 1917. For the complete listing of the books that are published by Yesterday's Classics, please visit www.yesterdaysclassics.com. Yesterday's Classics is the publishing arm of Gateway to the Classics which presents the complete text of hundreds of classic books for children at www.gatewaytotheclassics.com.

ISBN: 978-159915-465-7

Yesterday's Classics, LLC
PO Box 339
Ithaca, NY 14851

CONTENTS

CHAPTER I

THE LION

THE next animal that Tommy Smith had a conversation with was—the lion! You will see, from this, that he was not at home, in the country, any longer, because there are no lions to talk to in the woods and fields. The fact is, it was Christmas-time, and his parents had come with their family to spend a few weeks (or perhaps months) in London. In London, as you know, there is the Zoological Gardens, and of course Tommy Smith was very fond of going there. This was his first visit, and he found that the animals who lived there were as ready to talk to him as the ones at home had been. Perhaps they were even more glad of a chat. All that was necessary was that he should be by himself, because they wouldn't talk if there were other people there. But as Tommy Smith didn't want to talk to animals before other people, and as there was often nobody else to interrupt them, that made it all the better.

I am not quite sure whether it was the lion that first began the conversation with Tommy Smith, or Tommy Smith with the lion, only the first seems more likely, because for a little boy to begin a conversation with a lion would be a very bold thing to do. But anyhow, from the very first, the lion had an encouraging manner, and it was not long before he told Tommy Smith that he need not feel nervous in talking to him, because, after all, he was only just a great big cat.

"Are you really, Mr. Lion?" said Tommy Smith.

"To be sure I am," said the lion, "and so are the rest of us here. Why, what are the tiger and leopard, then, if they're not cats? I thought you knew that."

"Yes, I did know that they were, Mr. Lion," said Tommy Smith, "but then you don't look so much like a cat as they do."

"Why not?" said the lion.

"I suppose it's because you've got a mane, Mr. Lion," said Tommy Smith. "Cats that one has in houses never have manes, and none of the others here have."

"That's their misfortune," said the lion, "but it doesn't make any real difference. Why, what real difference would it make, if your hair was much longer than other boys' hair? You'd still be a boy, I suppose. The only difference would be that you'd be a handsomer boy. You see that, don't you?"

"Er—yes, Mr. Lion," said Tommy Smith. He saw the first part of it, at any rate.

"It's the same with me," said the lion. "I'm as much a cat as any of them, only I'm a handsomer one."

Tommy Smith thought that the tiger might think in the same way about his beautiful striped skin, and

The Lion

the leopard about his spotted one. Of course it was true that his mane made the lion very handsome, but he didn't think that it was a handsome way for him to talk about it, because the lioness had none. However, he saw what the lion meant, and he knew that he was a cat now, both because he said so, and because he began to remember that it said so in the natural history books too, which was just as if two very great learned judges were to be of the same opinion about something. But it was not quite so much what the lion was, as what he did, that Tommy Smith wanted to hear him talk about, so instead of waiting for his next remark (for he looked just as if he was going to say: "Yes, we all belong to the great cat family") he said: "Please, Mr. Lion, do tell me something about what you do when you're wild and not shut up in a cage."

"Cage!" said the lion indignantly. "My den, if you please. A nice thing it would be if a lion were shut up in his own den. It is mine. If anyone thinks it is not, let him try to turn me out of it—that's all. And as for anybody but me coming inside it, I allow nobody to, and that is so well understood that nobody ever tries to. So now I hope *you* understand."

Tommy Smith thought he did understand, for he felt quite sure that the poor lion did not like to think that he was shut up in a cage, and so pretended that he was in his own den. So as Tommy Smith was not too old to pretend, he pretended, too, and said: "Oh, yes, I see, Mr. Lion, but please tell me something about what you do when you're not in your den here, but in your own country."

"Well," said the lion, "I do a great many things, so where would like me to begin?"

"How do you kill animals, Mr. Lion?" said Tommy Smith, for he thought that would be the most interesting.

"Why, with my teeth and my claws, to be sure," the lion answered. "They were not made for nothing, you know."

"But I mean, Mr. Lion," said Tommy Smith, for this wasn't like telling about it, "when you see an animal and want to kill it, what do you do?"

"Why, it depends on what animal it is," said the lion. "I don't kill them all in just the same way."

"Supposing it was a buffalo, Mr. Lion," said Tommy Smith.

"I should have to be careful with him," said the lion, "especially if it were a bull. The first thing would be to creep up so near to him, without his knowing, that I should be able to rush in and seize him, before he had time to run away, when he saw me."

"I suppose you'd creep through the bushes, so that he couldn't see you, Mr. Lion," said Tommy Smith.

"That's all very well, when there are bushes all about," said the lion, "but sometimes there are only a few, or not any at all. Then, I must creep through the grass, if there is any, but in the winter it is poor and thin and that makes it more difficult for me. I press my body quite flat to the ground, and move along almost as if I were a snake. Every now and then, I stop and raise my head, just a little, so that I can peep through the grass, to see just where the buffalo that I am stalking is. But I soon bring it down again, and, all the time I'm not looking, I hold it as low as the rest of my body, or even lower."

"So that he shan't see you, Mr. Lion?" said Tommy Smith.

"Yes," said the lion, "and it isn't as if there was only one of them to think about, for buffaloes go in herds, and browse about in each other's company, so that even though there may be one, here or there, by itself, there are sure to be others, scattered about, that one has to get by."

"It must be difficult, Mr. Lion," said Tommy Smith.

"Yes, and what makes it hardest of all," said the lion, "is that if the wind should be behind me, it takes my scent to any animal in front of me, and then it runs away. Of course when one buffalo runs away, others that see it think there must be something the matter, so they go off too, and soon the whole herd is in motion."

"I wonder you ever get one, Mr. Lion," said Tommy Smith.

"Of course, I hide my scent when I can," said the lion, "by creeping up against the wind. When the wind's blowing from them to me, they can't scent me, and, almost always, I get up so close to the one I want, without his seeing me either, that I have time to make a great rush, and get hold of him, before he can get into full flight. You see, for a little while, I can gallop very fast indeed, faster than a horse even."

"Can you really, Mr. Lion?" said Tommy Smith. This was quite a surprise to him. "Oh, I wish I could see you."

"I wish you could," said the lion, in rather a sad tone of voice, Tommy Smith thought. "Yes," he continued, "my speed, for just a time, is tremendous, but it doesn't last long. It's just a rush, and after that, I can't go so fast even as a buffalo can. But often I don't have to make a rush at all. I creep up so quietly that I seem to rise out of the earth, just by the side of my quarry (that's the buffalo I'm stalking, of course), and in one moment, I have one of my paws over his shoulder and the other one on his nose, pulling his head down to the ground."

"But where are you, Mr. Lion?" asked Tommy Smith. "I mean," he explained, "how are you standing?"

"I'm not standing at all," said the lion, "I'm hanging

on to the buffalo, with my whole body underneath his, and my hind feet only just touching the ground."

"What, with your back to the ground, Mr. Lion?" said Tommy Smith. "I don't see what you can do like that."

"I don't have to do anything except hold on," said the lion, "and I do that well, till he falls down."

"But then he must fall on you, Mr. Lion," said Tommy Smith, "and if it was a buffalo——"

"It is a buffalo," said the lion, "and he does fall down, as I told you, but not on me. If he did, he would crush me or hurt me badly; but as he rushes along, trying to get away from me, and quite mad with fright, I keep dragging his head down between his forelegs, with my weight, till, at last, he loses his balance and stumbles and down he comes, with his head under him, so that he turns right over in the air, and lies on his back, right in front of me. But I still have my paw in his muzzle, with my sharp claws sticking into it, and, as I scramble up, with my powerful forearm I give his head a tremendous wrench round to one side, so that the neck is broken, and, after that, it's all fun and feasting."

Tommy Smith thought that there was not much fun about it for the buffalo, but he knew it would be no good to explain that there wasn't, and besides, he hardly felt big enough to explain things like that to a lion. He felt very sorry for the buffalo, but then he knew that lions and tigers had to eat other animals, and that they must be large animals because they were so large themselves, and one could hardly expect them to be sorry about it; and, even if they were, that would not make it any better for the animals they killed. And then, too, he remembered that there were ladies who seemed to think it fun to see a cat playing with a mouse, though the only difference between the two things was that the mouse was smaller, and that the cat took much longer in killing it than the lion seemed to take in killing a buffalo. So he thought it would be better and much more sensible, to be angry with these ladies than with any lion or tiger. And besides, if it came to that, he might just as well feel angry with himself, whenever he ate beef or mutton, because, although he didn't kill the ox or the sheep that it came from, yet somebody else killed them for him. So all he said was: "I think it's very clever of you, Mr. Lion, and you must be very strong to be able to do it. But doesn't the buffalo sometimes hurt you with his horns, because, you know, he's very strong too?"

"If it comes to that," said the lion, "he's great deal stronger than I am. He's so much bigger, you see, only besides my strength, which is very great for my size, I have four other things, my skill, my courage, my teeth, and my claws. All these together make me able to manage cow-buffaloes, or bulls that have not got their full size and strength; but an old bull is a different thing, and I generally leave him alone."

"But don't you always, then, Mr. Lion?" said Tommy Smith.

"Why, of course, if I was very hungry," said the lion, "and could find no other game———"

"Do you mean no other animals, Mr. Lion?" said Tommy Smith.

"Yes, that's what I mean," said the lion. "I speak like a sportsman, because I am one. If I could find no other game, as I say, and was very hungry, there's no saying what I mightn't do; only if I were alone, I should be carrying my life in my claws. The best way, with an old buffalo, is to make a family affair of it."

"What do you mean by that, Mr. Lion?" asked Tommy Smith.

At this moment the lioness came stealing out of what was really the den (however the lion might talk about it), through a small square opening in the wall at the back of the cage. She looked as if she had been asleep, but, at any rate, she must have heard the last part of the conversation, for she said at once: "Why, that his wife and children help him, to be sure. That's what he means, and so they do, very often."

"Very true, my dear," said the lion, "and you know how grateful I am to you all."

"Not always," said the lioness. "Sometimes you snarl at us for wanting our share."

"Only just at first, when I'm excited," said the lion. "We soon settle down to a quite friendly family meal, and even when you and your cubs have not helped me at all, I've often stood with my two fore-paws on the carcass, and roared loudly till you all came running up to share it with me."

"But do the cubs really help to kill buffaloes, Mrs. Lioness?" said Tommy Smith.

"After they're not quite little they do," said the lioness. "That's how we teach them their business in life. They stay with us for two years, and sometimes longer, and we give them the best of educations."

"I suppose you mean in killing animals," said Tommy Smith.

"Oh, yes,—it's practical," said the lion.

"No use filling their heads with things they don't really require," said the lioness.

"What other animals do you kill, Mr. Lion?" asked Tommy Smith.

"Almost all that there are in the country I live in, which is Africa," said the lion, "because I'm the African lion. But antelopes and zebras are my favourites. They're not so difficult to kill. A bite or two in the neck, behind the ears, would be enough for most of them, but sometimes one has to be careful about the horns. Have you heard of the gemsbuck?"

"Oh, yes I have, Mr. Lion," said Tommy Smith, "and I've seen its picture in natural history books. It's a beautiful antelope that runs very fast, about as large as a pony—I mean quite a small pony. It's black and white, I think, Mr. Lion, at least its head is, and its horns are very long and quite straight, and——"

"The worst horns there are," said the lion.

"Oh, those horrid long horns with points as sharp

as a needle," said the lioness. "They'd go right through one if——"

"They do sometimes," said the lion. "Our two bleached skeletons have been found fixed together like that."

"Then did you kill each other, Mr. Lion?" asked Tommy Smith.

"We did—it was a tragedy," said the lion. "I stalked him, and flung myself upon him, with my right paw over his right shoulder. But before I could bite him behind the ears, which would have been the end of him, he flung back his head—I suppose in a frenzy of terror—and those terrible horns were driven almost through the length of my body."

"It was some other lion's body, really, you know, Mr. Lion," said Tommy Smith, "because you're still alive."

"It might have been mine," said the lion, "and when I tell the story I feel as if it was."

"Do you ever kill giraffes, Mr. Lion?" was Tommy Smith's next question.

"Sometimes I do," said the lion, "but not very often. You see, they're so tall. Beautiful necks! They make one feel hungry. But then it's like climbing up a tree. As for the bulls—I mean the males—they're almost too strong for me, but, from time to time, I kill a cow or a young one."

"Sometimes we pull one down together, you know," said the lioness. "We might get a grown-up bull then."

"They grow up so high," said the lion, "and they do plunge and shake so, even cows."

"Still, together——" urged the lioness.

"Together we might do wonders," said the lion, with an affectionate glance at his partner. "But then, dear, they get into the thirst country, where we can't live. We lions, you know, must have water."

"But can giraffes live without water?" asked Tommy Smith.

"Much better than we can," answered the lion. "They go right away into the sandy desert, and if they get any water at all, for months as a time, I think it must be from the melons that grow all about there."

"But can't you, too, Mr. Lion?" said Tommy Smith.

"Certainly not," said the lioness. "Lions can't live upon melons."

"But, if they've got water inside them, Mrs. Lioness," said Tommy Smith, "why——?"

"I've told you the reason," said the lioness. "Lions can't live upon melons."

"Impossible," said the lion; "so that makes another reason why we can't live on giraffes either. It's a pity, for they certainly have beautiful necks."

"Never mind, dear," said the lioness. "So have ostriches."

"True, true," said the lion, "and just one bite is sufficient with them."

"But can you catch an ostrich, Mr. Lion?" asked Tommy Smith, "because, you know, they run so fast. Faster than a horse," he added, for he had always heard that.

"We don't try to race them," said the lion; "but there's a way of doing things, and we manage to get a few now and then. Do we not, dear?"

"We know what they taste like," said the lioness.

"You see, they're not nocturnal, as we are," the lion explained (Tommy Smith knew what "nocturnal" meant quite well, because the barn-owl had told him), "so they have to sit down somewhere at night, and sometimes we take them by surprise."

"How the feathers do fly, when we do," said the lioness.

"And how soon it's all over," said the lion. "Yes, they have nice necks, and how they do crunch."

Tommy Smith felt sorry for the poor ostriches, but as they were caught suddenly, at night, and as just one bite of the neck was sufficient to kill them—as the lion said—he thought it must be better for them than for the poor buffaloes and antelopes. But he had heard enough now about how the lion killed animals, so he thought he would ask him some questions of a different kind. "Please, Mr. Lion," he said, "will you tell me something about the people you live amongst in Africa—I mean who live in Africa too? I suppose they're black people."

"Some are," said the lion, "but where I'm most common, they're not black, but brown. Those are the

13

Kaffirs, and I don't so much mind living near them, because they keep cattle. They're very fond of cattle, and we're very fond of them too."

"I suppose you like living near them, because you kill their cattle, Mr. Lion?" said Tommy Smith.

"That's the best part of it," said the lion, "but accidents happen."

"Very disagreeable ones," said the lioness. "It would be better to leave them alone."

"But aren't they easier to kill than buffaloes, Mr. Lion?" said Tommy Smith.

"Much," said the lion.

"We don't mind them," said the lioness.

Tommy Smith saw that it was another sort of accident the lions were thinking of. "Are the Kaffirs angry when you kill their cattle, Mr. Lion?" he asked.

"Very," said the lion.

"Very angry, indeed," said the lioness. And there was rather a long pause after that, for neither of them seemed inclined to say anything more, so that Tommy Smith didn't quite know how to go on.

"Do they do anything, Mr. Lion?" he asked at last.

"They kill us," said the lion. "That's what they do."

"That's all," said the lioness. And they both looked very cross and discontented.

"But how can they kill you, Mr. Lion?" asked Tommy

Smith. "Because you're so strong and so fierce, you know."

"I dare say I am," said the lion, a little surlily, "but I can't win a fight against a nation. I'm not strong enough for that, and, as for fierceness, no one could be fiercer than those brown men with their assegais. That's what they call their spears, you know."

"Yes, and with their shields," said the lioness. "They wouldn't be so fierce if they hadn't those great shields to fight behind. All *we* have is our own teeth and claws."

"One naked lion," said the lion, in a grumbling tone of voice, "against weapons and numbers. No, I can't fight a nation in arms."

"You do," said the lioness, with a look of pride at her husband.

"Anyhow, I can't win," said the lion.

"Oh, do please tell me about it, Mr. Lion," said Tommy Smith.

"What generally happens is this," said the lion. "I just kill one single ox, and when I have had a reasonable meal, I go to sleep somewhere near it. Then all the fighting men from everywhere round, each carrying a shield and assegai, march up to where I lie. They tread softly, so as not to wake me, and spread round me on every side, so that when I do wake up, I find myself in the centre of a circle of men. Whichever way I turn there are spears and shields, with tall savages behind them, thirsting for my blood. And now, as I stand growling fiercely, with eyes blazing and tail lashing my sides, the circle begins to close in on me, so that it gets narrower and narrower. Then, all at once, before I can make up my mind where to try to break through, one of the men who has been chosen for his strength and ferocity—the greatest ruffian of the gang—starts out, alone, before the rest, and rushes straight at me, calling me names and insulting me."

"What does he call you, Mr. Lion?" asked Tommy Smith.

"Oh, a thief and a vagabond, and all sorts of other disgraceful names," said the lion; "perhaps a murderer even, just as if a lion could live without killing his dinner. And it's not only myself that he abuses in this shameful way, but my family and all my ancestors, going right back, ever so far. Of course, I rush upon my reviler, but just as I get within striking distance, he sinks down beneath that great shield of his and stabs up at me from under it. I do my best to dash it aside, and often get my teeth through his arm or his shoulder, but all his friends rush in so quickly that, almost as I seize hold of him, a dozen or twenty assegais are quivering in my body or driven right through me."

"Oh, poor Mr. Lion," said Tommy Smith. "Then I suppose they kill you."

"Always—I told you so," said the lion, with a pained expression. "If I did not accept the challenge of the man who runs out at me, I might break through the circle and get away. But that would not be courageous, so, of course, I always do accept it; and whilst I am occupied with my principal enemy, all the rest come up and kill me."

"Never mind, dear," said the lioness. "You die like a hero."

"I know that, of course," said the lion, "but it's very unjust. And then there are the Bushmen."

"Oh, do tell me about them, Mr. Lion," said Tommy Smith, for he had heard about the Bushmen, and was interested in them.

"They're worse," said the lion, "for they don't keep oxen, and so can't pretend that they're injured. But that doesn't matter. Whenever they see me lying asleep—even if I haven't killed anything—they creep up as close as they can to me, and shoot me with one of those poisoned arrows of theirs."

"Horrid things!" said the lioness.

"Does the poison kill you, Mr. Lion?" said Tommy Smith.

"What a question!" said the lion. "Why, the Bushman poison kills everything. And yet one would hardly believe it. It isn't as if it were an assegai that goes right through one, very often, but just a thin reed, not so long as your arm, with a little piece of bone at the end. A sort of toy arrow it looks like, and yet it kills me."

"But does it go through your skin, Mr. Lion?" said Tommy Smith.

"It goes into it, anyhow," said the lion, "and that's enough with a poisoned arrow."

"It does its work," said the lioness, and then there was another rather long pause. It seemed as if it was too painful a subject for either of them to want to talk about, but Tommy Smith didn't think it was properly finished yet, so, after a little, he asked: "Does it wake you up, Mr. Lion?"

"Yes, indeed," said the lion. "It pricks me, so, of course, I wake; and when I see something hanging to me, I'm surprised and jump up, and bound away. Perhaps I make a bite at it first, but, whether I do or not, the shaft of the arrow—the reed part, I mean—soon breaks off, but the bone head, with the poison on it, still sticks where it was, because it's made in such a way that it can't come out."

"Oh, is it barbed, Mr. Lion?" said Tommy Smith.

"I dare say that's what you'd call it," said the lion. "All I know is that it won't come out, and those cruel little yellow men make it like that on purpose."

"Just to torture us," said the lioness—and she looked very fierce.

"Such puny creatures, too," said the lion. "That seems to make it worse."

"Yes, and so ugly," said the lioness. "Little yellow men with eyes like slits, and hair that doesn't curl properly, because there isn't enough of it."

"And yet they kill us," said the lion. "What a puzzle it all is."

"I suppose the poisoned arrow begins to hurt you soon, Mr. Lion," said Tommy Smith.

"Dreadfully," said the lion, "dreadfully." Then he gave a few low growls, and so did the lioness, after which they were both silent again.

"How does it go on, please, Mr. Lion?" said Tommy Smith, after he had waited a little.

"Very badly indeed," said the lion, whilst the lioness put her face between her paws, and looked another way. "I told you that it pricks me at first, and how I wake up and bound away. Of course, the pain of a prick is not much—nothing to a lion—only one expects it to go. But it doesn't go. Instead of that, it gets worse, and very soon I'm suffering the most horrible torture."

"Where, Mr. Lion?" asked Tommy Smith.

"Oh, all over me," said the lion. "It's a dreadful burning heat that seems to scorch up my blood, and I get dreadfully thirsty and go to the nearest water, and lap and lap and lap at it, as if that were the only way to feel as I used to, again. But I never do any more. It doesn't do me any good at all. It's as if a great fire were burning inside me which all the water of the country could never put out, and this fire gets hotter and hotter, and dreadful pains keep shooting through me as well; and I get so weak, at last, I can't even drink any more, but just lie on the ground, moaning and biting at the grass, or at sticks or anything."

"Don't go on, dear," said the lioness, "it's too painful." And then she looked a little reproachfully at Tommy Smith, and said: "I don't think you ought to want him to."

"Oh, no, I don't, Mrs. Lioness," said Tommy Smith,

"only——Please, how long does it last, Mr. Lion?" He couldn't help asking, because it was so interesting.

"Oh, a horrible time," said the lion with great feeling. "I don't quite know, only, however long it is, it seems ever so much longer. All I can tell you is that it's the longest thing I've ever had anything to do with; and then, at last, I die, and those little fiends of yellow men follow up my track, and find me lying on my side—still warm perhaps—and begin to skin me. Such an indignity! It's a good the thing the breath is out of my body, for I should feel it more than anything, if it were not."

Tommy Smith certainly thought that being skinned alive might be even more painful than being shot with a poisoned arrow, but he knew what the lion meant. "It is a shame, Mr. Lion," he said.

"It's bad enough, I think," the lion continued, "to be run through with twenty or thirty assegais, perhaps, so as to look more like a porcupine than a lion—of course a much larger and nobler porcupine. But, after all, one may kill two or three of those big brown men—the Kaffirs—if one's lucky, and perhaps wound a great many more. That's something. But to have a wretched little yellow dwarf creeping up to one whilst one's asleep, and shooting one with poisoned arrows, so that one dies slowly, in agony, without ever seeing him even, is ever so much worse. It's too bad."

"So it is, dear," said the lioness, "but don't get too excited about it. Remember, I've suffered as much as you."

"Why were they made?" said the lion (he didn't

seem at all comforted by this remark of the lioness).
"There's very little meat on them, and even if there were
more, one can't often get it—they're so cunning. They're
no good to lions. Then why were they made?"

"Don't you think, dear," said the lioness, "that if you
were to have a good roar—a thorough good roar now—
you'd feel better after it?"

The lion shook his head and muttered something
which sounded like "Nonsense."

"It's such a relief," urged the lioness.

"It does something, of course," said the lion, "but it
doesn't answer questions."

But whatever it did or did not do, the lion meant to
do it, for when he had said this, he got up—he had been
lying down for some little time—opened his mouth—
but not quite so wide as in yawning—and gave several
deep roars, one after the other, with very short pauses
between them. It was a long, deep, rolling sound which
grew louder and deeper as it went on, till the whole air
trembled (and so did Tommy Smith, too, a little), and
all the more when the lioness joined in and began to
roar too—then, of course, it was tremendous. At the
beginning of each roar, both the great cats lowered their
heads, and then raised them again as it went on, as if
to fling out the sound, and they certainly did fling it
out. They both of them looked very grand as they did
this, but the lion, of course, looked much the grander of
the two, because of his mane. "There!" said the lioness,
after the concert had come to an end. "We both of us
feel better now, I dare say. Nothing like a good roar for

getting rid of disturbing thoughts. After all, if it were not for Bushmen, lions might grow too proud. Well"—this was to Tommy Smith—"what do you think of it?"

"Oh, I think it's splendid, Mrs. Lioness," said Tommy Smith. "You *do* make a noise."

The lion tossed his mane, and the lioness her head (as she had only that). Somehow neither of them looked as if they were quite satisfied with this remark, only Tommy Smith didn't know why, because, of course, it was a noise. The lioness was just beginning with: "Well, really——" but the lion looked at her in a way that made her stop, and said: "No, dear, he's only a child," which Tommy Smith thought rather curious, because there was no doubt at all about that. Then he gave a grand sort of smile at Tommy Smith, and said: "Of course, you will understand that this is music which sounds better in the wilderness."

"So does thunder," said the lioness; "but perhaps you would call that 'a noise.'"

"Thunder has been compared to *our* thunder," said the lion, "and perhaps there is some faint resemblance."

"Very faint," said the lioness.

"Only, of course," the lion added, "it must be right overhead."

"And very low down," said the lioness. "If not, we should drown it."

"Yes," continued the lion, "it's then that you ought to hear us, when the sun sinks and night comes down over the great African waste. That's the time for us to roar, under a million bright twinkling stars, ever so much brighter than they are here, and the moon, when she rises, is like a pale sun, but not so pale as this one. Only we roar most when it's as black and dark as the night, without the moon, can make it. No one can see us then, as we prowl about, and we lions, when we roar, like to be heard but not seen."

"Do you roar louder then, Mr. Lion?" said Tommy Smith.

"Oh, much," said the lion. "You see, here, the damp air is bad for our lungs, but there it's a dry climate."

"Tell him how we roar against each other," said the lioness.

"That's the finest of all," said the lion. "When one of us begins, another answers, perhaps from quite a long way off, so that it only sounds faintly, but, before long, another of us, from somewhere between, answers him; and so it goes on, nearer or farther away, rumbling all round the horizon, and over the forests and hills and plains, lion against lion, thunder answering thunder."

"It must sound splendid, Mr. Lion," said Tommy Smith.

"Oh, grand, grand," said the lion, with a much more satisfied smile. "But we've something even beyond that. The grandest of all is when we roar in troops, and one troop—a troop of lions—answers another troop."

"But do lions go in troops?" asked Tommy Smith.

"Anyhow, we go in families," the lion answered, "and sometimes there are a few more than just the family.

There may be eight or nine, or, sometimes, even a dozen of us together. That may not be a large troop, but if you were to meet it, one day, all of a sudden, without any idea beforehand that you were going to, I dare say you would find it quite large enough."

Tommy Smith thought he would find it quite large enough, even if he had had an idea beforehand that he was going to meet it, and he said so to the lion.

"Well, we all roar together," said the lion, "and when another troop hears us, they all roar together too. Try to imagine the effect."

Tommy Smith did try, and he thought that the lion had described it very well indeed, when he said: "Oh, grand, grand!" But there was one question he wanted to ask: "Please, Mr. Lion," he said, "when you roar so, don't all the animals that are afraid of you go right away? And then, how do you kill them for your dinner?"

"Oh, but it's after we've had our dinner that we roar like that," the lion answered. "When we're hungry, and still have it to catch, we're quiet enough. But when we have eaten as much as we want, then we march down to the nearest water, to drink, and on the way, every now and then, we stop on purpose to roar, and you should hear us then. Ah, those are the concerts of the desert."

"Why do you roar so much then, Mr. Lion?" asked Tommy Smith.

"Because, we're so happy," said the lion. "You see, we've eaten as much as we want to eat, and we're just on the way to drink as much as we want to drink. There

24

could hardly be a happier state than that for a lion to be in, so our hearts go out in joy and thankfulness—and we roar. It's a high feeling—perhaps as high a one as mere lions can have."

"There's the feeling one has just after pulling something down, before beginning to eat it, you know," said the lioness. "Isn't that a higher one still, dear?"

"I don't know," said the lion. "We don't roar so much then."

"Well, if you make that the test," said the lioness thoughtfully.

Tommy Smith didn't know which of the two feelings was the higher one, because he wasn't a lion, but he thought that whatever made lions roar most, was the most interesting. "I should like to hear you, Mr. Lion," he said,—"I mean where you live," he added, because, of course, he had just been hearing both of them.

"You might be frightened if you did," said the lion. "Supposing you were camping out, one night, on the banks of some African river, with hardly any fire, because it had been raining, and you couldn't get the wood to burn—and, all at once, you heard us roar like that, in the distance, and then, after a few minutes, nearer, and then nearer still, and always getting nearer and nearer, as we came down to the water, till at last we seemed to be passing right by you, though you couldn't see us, because the night was so dark—and then, if, between the intervals of our roaring, you heard us lapping the water, just below where you sat, and there was a hiss after every roar, as we drew in our breath like this,"—and the lion made the sound—"wouldn't you be very frightened?"

"Yes, I think I should be, Mr. Lion," said Tommy Smith.

"Then we agree with each other," said the lion, "so that makes a good place for finishing the conversation."

And without saying anything else, the lion paced slowly across the floor of his cage, and disappeared through the square opening, followed by the lioness.

CHAPTER II

THE EMPEROR PENGUIN

TOMMY SMITH felt so encouraged at having had a conversation with the lion that now he wanted to have one with the elephant. But on his way to the tunnel—for he had been told to go through the tunnel to get to the elephants—he came to a little plot of grass that had a path and then a railing round it, and there was a stone tank of water in the middle that looked rather large for a bath, but not large enough for a swimming-bath. Beside it, a little group of such funny birds were standing, quite upright, as if they were people, and Tommy Smith knew at once that they were penguins because he had read about them, and seen the pictures of some of them in natural history books. But one of them was much handsomer and very much larger than the others, and this one looked at Tommy Smith, as he was going by, in a way that there was no mistaking, and made him a very low bow. It was really a wonderful bow, for the bird brought its head right down till its beak and chin were pressed against the front of its body. It was easy to see that if it had been wearing a hat, it would have taken it off, at the same time, and held it nearly touching the ground, for that was just the attitude it stood in. Of course, Tommy Smith felt obliged to bow, too, only he couldn't do it nearly so well, and then the penguin bowed again, still lower than before, and said: "Here we are, all waiting for a conversation, only, as Emperor, I come first, of course."

"Emperor, Mr. Penguin?" cried Tommy Smith. He was surprised, as you may think.

"Yes, and not a common kind of one, either," said the penguin. "There's no other that's at all like me."

"But how are you an emperor, Mr. Penguin?" asked Tommy Smith.

"I'm more than *an* emperor," said the penguin. "Just to be *an* emperor would not be so remarkable. But I'm more than that, because I'm *the* Emperor Penguin." And, with this, there was another bow.

"Oh, I see, that's your name, Mr. Penguin," said Tommy Smith.

"If you think so, you should call me by it," said the emperor penguin. "But it's my name and my title both; and now that you know them both, I shall expect you to say them together."

"Oh, yes, I will, Mr. Emperor Penguin," said Tommy Smith, "but I think it's only your name."

"It must be either one or the other," said the emperor penguin, "so, if you don't say them both together, you will be leaving out either the whole of my title, or the half of my name. Either would be ill-bred."

The Emperor Penguin

"I wasn't going to leave either of them out, and I said I wasn't, Mr. Emperor Penguin," said Tommy Smith.

"I'm glad I've convinced you," said the emperor penguin.

"I suppose it's because you're *called* the emperor penguin," said Tommy Smith (he wanted him to understand that he knew he wasn't one really), "that you bow in that grand sort of way."

"To my equals in rank I do," said the emperor penguin, "but not to anyone else, except as a condescension."

Then, before Tommy Smith (who understood what he meant, although "condescension" was a long word) could say anything, he turned to the others who were standing a little behind him, and said, quite as grandly as he had bowed, "You may all retire."

On this, the other penguins made *their* bow, which was a much more ordinary one, and walked—or rather hopped, for that was their way of going fast—to the farther side of the enclosure. They did not seem at all offended, but Tommy Smith thought it was a shame. "You're all of you penguins, you know," he couldn't help saying.

"But not all emperors," said the emperor penguin quickly, and then added: "You see I'm going to be quite chatty and familiar with you, only when one has a position to keep up one should not relax too publicly. They won't notice anything from where they are."

At first Tommy Smith felt almost inclined to be angry with this, but afterwards he thought it was only funny, which was a much more sensible way of looking at it. After all, if the penguin couldn't get over his name, and thought himself an emperor when he was only just a bird, that was only a curious idea of his which did no harm to anybody. Perhaps, too, his appearance was some excuse for his thinking so, for he was really a very magnificent bird. His breast, which, of course, as he stood upright, was very conspicuous, and his throat, too, was of a beautiful lemon-yellow colour, and so smooth and glossy that it shone in the sun like satin. Lower down the feathers were white, and not yellow, but the one colour passed gradually into the other, and the whole effect was very fine. All the front and top part of the emperor penguin's head was of a rich velvety black, but on each side of it there was a patch of the beautiful yellow, and, just where this came highest up, the colour grew deeper, until it was quite golden and looked like a little sun. Then the under part of his bill was a beautiful pinky-red, and it looked all the brighter because the tip and the upper part were only brown. His back was not black, like his head, and it could hardly be called blue either, but there was both black and blue in it, and they were so mixed and dappled together that sometimes it looked almost black and sometimes almost blue. As for his wings, they were not at all like the wings of another bird, because their feathers were so short and smooth that they did not look like feathers at all, but much more like scales; but that was because a penguin's wings are used for swimming, and not for flying. They were funny wings, certainly, but Tommy Smith thought that the emperor penguin held them in a graceful manner; and there was great dignity, too, in the way he stood, and all the more so because he was three and half feet high. It even seemed to Tommy Smith (though, of course, it was a childish idea) that some real emperors might not be so handsome and grand-looking as this very handsome emperor penguin, and although the next thing he said was only: "What a funny bird you are, Mr. Emperor Penguin," that was not quite all that he meant, so that when the answer came, as it did directly: "Handsome I suppose you mean," he said at once: "Yes, Mr. Emperor Penguin, I meant that, too."

"Always say what you mean, said the emperor penguin. "As for my being handsome, everyone, of course, can see that, but what there is funny about me I'm sure I don't know."

"But you do stand and walk in a funny way, Mr. Emperor Penguin," said Tommy Smith. "I mean for a bird," he explained.

"For what bird?" said the emperor penguin. "Not for a penguin, I hope."

"Oh, no, not for a penguin, of course, Mr. Emperor Penguin," said Tommy Smith, "but—but for any other kind of bird, you know."

"As for that," said the emperor penguin, "you might just as well say that any other kind of bird stood and walked in a funny way for a penguin. And so it does."

"Yes, but then other birds are not penguins, you know, Mr. Emperor Penguin," said Tommy Smith.

"And penguins are not other birds, thank goodness," said the emperor penguin: "so it's no use trying to get out of it in that way."

Tommy Smith felt sure he was right, only perhaps he had not explained it properly. "But you see you're so different from other birds, Mr. Emperor Penguin," he began again. "That's what makes you look funny. No other bird walks in the way that you do. Only, of course, it's a very good way," he added, for the penguin began to look ruffled. "And then almost all other birds fly, and you don't fly, because your wings——"

"Almost all, did you say?" said the emperor penguin. "Then are there any besides us who don't?"

"Oh, yes, Mr. Emperor Penguin," said Tommy Smith. "There's the ostrich—he can't fly, of course—and the emu and rhea can't either, and no more can the cassowary, or——"

"Dear me, you surprise me," said the emperor penguin. "But I live so out of the world. Why, I don't know their names even. But I'm glad to think the world does move on."

"Do you mean that it's better not to fly, Mr. Emperor Penguin?" said Tommy Smith.

"Much more sensible," said the emperor penguin. "And so we penguins have left it off altogether."

"But did you fly once, then, Mr. Emperor Penguin?" said Tommy Smith.

"A long time ago we did," said the emperor penguin, "but we grew more and more ashamed of such a silly flighty habit, and so we gave it up. No penguin would think of flying now."

"Yes, but that's because you can't, Mr. Emperor Penguin," said Tommy Smith. "Your wings haven't got any feathers on them—at least, I mean not any long feathers. They couldn't hold you up without those, you know, and so you wouldn't be able to fly now, even if you were to try to."

"Thank goodness for that," said the emperor penguin. "It was not always so, as I told you. For a very long time, the wings of our ancestors still had those nasty long spikey things which, I suppose, is what you mean. It seemed as if we'd never get rid of them. But as we grew more and more accustomed to the water, they got shorter and shorter, till at last what had been the mere clumsy wing of a bird was improved into the true penguin paddle or flipper—that wonderful instrument— which I here have the honour of presenting to you." And the emperor penguin made another low bow and put out his right flipper (or paddle) between the bars of the railings (for he had come up to them) for Tommy Smith to look at. Of course, Tommy Smith did look at it (he even shook it), and, the more he did, the more wonderful it seemed to him that it could ever have been a wing, like another bird's.

"It seems very funny for it to have changed, Mr. Emperor Penguin," he said.

"It took a very long time," said the emperor penguin. "Oh, ages. It seemed as if it *never* would come. But you see it has come—there it is—and it's the greatest comfort in the world, now, to be able to think that no penguin, even if he were to wish it, can be betrayed into habits of flight."

Tommy Smith couldn't help feeling surprised at what the emperor penguin had told him, but that a bird should not want to fly, and even talk as though flying were silly, didn't surprise him at all, because he had found out that animals always thought that whatever they did was just the right thing to do, and whatever they didn't do, the wrong thing. Of course, it was funny, but Tommy Smith could always explain it by saying to himself that they were animals and not people. So instead of trying to show the penguin how wrong his ideas were, as he would have done if he had been a person instead of just a bird, he only said: "I suppose you can swim very fast in the water, Mr. Emperor Penguin?"

"I should think so," said the penguin; "a great deal faster I'm sure that you could run on the ice, if you wanted to race me like that."

"I couldn't run very fast on the ice," said Tommy Smith, "because I should slip and fall down. It would have to be the land for me to run on, and I think you ought to run on it, too. Then, it would be a fair race."

"As fair as if you were to swim me," said the emperor penguin. "But I wouldn't mind trying on the ice. The ice is my land. I live in the Antarctic Ocean, and whatever is not ice, there, is sea, and whatever is not sea, is ice."

"But isn't there any land at all, Mr. Emperor Penguin?" said Tommy Smith.

"It's only ice that I go on," said the emperor penguin, "and when I want to catch fish I dive into the sea, through a hole in it. One can't do that here, so I suppose what you call the land is a sort of bad ice, which I consider this to be (by 'this' the penguin meant the ground). But if you wanted to race me in that way, it would have to be upon the good ice, and that would only be fair, because it's what I've always been accustomed to."

Tommy Smith didn't think it would be quite fair to him, because he was much more accustomed to run upon dry ground. But even upon ice he thought he would run faster than the penguin, because of his much longer legs and the longer strides he could take with them; and even if he did fall down sometimes, it wouldn't take him long to get up again. So he told him that he would be ready to race him on the ice, too, if ever they were on it together.

"Well," said the emperor penguin, "you'd have to go at about ten miles an hour, to beat me. That's all."

"Ten miles an hour, Mr. Emperor Penguin!" cried Tommy Smith. (He could hardly believe it.) "Surely you can't run so fast as that."

"Run!" said the penguin. "I should not run. I should toboggan."

"Toboggan? Oh, but how would you do that, Mr. Emperor Penguin?" asked Tommy Smith. He had heard of tobogganing in Canada, and even done a little of it himself, too, in England.

"Yes," continued the emperor penguin, "that is what I should do, and then I would glide over the ice at such a rate that I should soon get ahead of you, and I don't believe you would ever catch me up."

"Oh, but then, have you a sledge, Mr. Emperor Penguin?" said Tommy Smith. Of course that didn't seem probable, but what else could he mean?

"A sledge! Why, whatever are you talking about?" said the emperor penguin, not at all in a pleased tone of voice. "I've nothing to do with sledges, and I wish they'd nothing to do with me. Don't talk to me about them, please, for they bring the men to my country who are always interfering with me, and even go so far as to kill me and eat me, which is a shocking way of treating an emperor. Let me hear nothing more of sledges, I beg."

"But you said you tobogganed, Mr. Emperor Penguin," said Tommy Smith, "and one does use a sledge, or at least a kind of one, for that, you know. It's a little thing made of wood, that you sit on, with your legs out on each side, and slide down the hills when there's snow on them."

"A clumsy imitation," said the emperor penguin. "When we penguins toboggan, we go down on our breasts, on the ice and push ourselves along, over it, with our legs and wings. That's our tobogganing. We're our own sledges, and I wish no other ones ever came into my country."

"Oh, I see now, Mr. Emperor Penguin," said Tommy Smith. "Only I thought penguins always walked upright."

"That's our favourite way when we're left alone," said the emperor penguin. "Nothing can be more graceful and dignified" (here the penguin made a little promenade over the ground just to show Tommy Smith, and really he did walk in a quite stately manner); "only when we're interfered with—as we have been since those sledges have come—it usen't to be so before—we try to go as fast as we can, so as to get away, and then we toboggan."

"I should like to see you do that as well, Mr. Emperor Penguin," said Tommy Smith.

"How can I on ice like this?" said the emperor penguin, with a glance round about him. "I couldn't possibly do myself justice if I were to try to. Such bad ice is really not fit for tobogganing."

But, for all that, the penguin did try to, after a little, and though, of course, it was much more difficult for him than if he had been on the ice in his own country, still he got along quite well enough to show Tommy Smith how it was done. In doing this, his beautiful white and yellow breast became all soiled with mud, so that if he had got up, at once, he would not have looked nearly so handsome a bird, but, instead of that, he pushed himself along into his little basin of water, and gave himself a good wash there, before coming out again.

"Oh, thank you, Mr. Emperor Penguin," said Tommy Smith. "It is kind of you. Now I know what tobogganing is with penguins, and I never should have done, properly, if I hadn't seen it."

"It's the only right way," said the emperor penguin, "and, now you know it, you must promise me always to practice it. I have done my best to show you, and that is all I ask from you in return. I have suffered so much from sledges that I don't like to think of any friend of mine using one."

Tommy Smith didn't quite know what to say to this, in fact he felt very much embarrassed, only luckily the penguin went on without waiting, so that he hadn't to say anything, and of course when one hasn't said anything one hasn't promised.

"I would show you the right way to swim too,"—that was how the emperor penguin went on,—"if only the sea here were large enough, but somehow it isn't. How it comes to be so small I don't know."

"It isn't the sea, Mr. Emperor Penguin," said Tommy Smith. "It's only a sort of basin that's been made for you."

"A bay I suppose you mean," said the emperor penguin. "Only that's just a part of the sea, and where should the rest of it have got to? It's the sea, of course— all water is the sea—but why it's so small, and what's become of the ice that there ought to be in it, I'm sure I don't know. As for it's having been made for me, that may be true. I can believe that part of your story. The beautiful sea that I used to have, that was so large and had everything I wanted in it, was made for me—at least I have always supposed so. But when things are made for emperors they ought to be made properly, and a sea that one can only just wash in is not large enough. Besides, there are no fish or anything else to eat in it, so that I call it a thoroughly bad sea—quite unworthy of an emperor penguin."

Tommy Smith could understand the penguin's making the mistakes that he did, because until he came away from where he used to live, he had never seen any water that was not the sea, or been on any land that was not ice. So after all, it was natural, even if he had been a person; but that he should think that all the ice and sea had been made for him was one of those queer sort of conceited ideas that animals had. Tommy Smith knew that there would be no getting that out of his head, and besides, it would be difficult to prove. As for those other things he was wrong about, he thought he might be able to explain them to him, only another day (for of course he meant to come again) would do as well, or even better, because now he wanted to get on with the conversation.

"Do you catch a great many fish, to eat, Mr. Emperor Penguin?" was the next question that Tommy Smith asked.

"Why, it's my principal occupation," the emperor penguin answered, "at least for all the year round. Of course there are the domestic duties, which are higher, but they don't go on for such a time. To catch and eat fish is always a duty."

"I suppose you like eating them, Mr. Emperor Penguin?" said Tommy Smith, who thought this rather a high way of talking.

"I should think I did," said the emperor penguin, "and so I do catching them. In fact I hardly know which is the higher pleasure of the two."

Tommy Smith didn't either, so he only said: "Isn't it very difficult for you to catch them, Mr. Emperor Penguin?"

"Difficult! What can you mean?" said the emperor penguin. "It's almost *too* easy for a duty. Oh, the dear little shining silver things, how they do shoot about when I come amongst them! It's the prettiest sight in the world. They do hurry and scurry so, all trying to get out of my way. So polite, but it's no use. It's just 'Here you *are*,' 'Down you *go*,' 'Pray don't *hurry*,' 'Now, can't I persuade *you?*' 'Thank you, you are so very nice,' with one after another of them, till I've had as many as I want. Oh, the dear little silver things. I do like them so."

"I think it is very funny that you catch them so easily, Mr. Emperor Penguin," said Tommy Smith, "because you see they are fish, and you're only a bird in the water."

"It would seem very funny to me," said the penguin, "if I couldn't catch them as easily as I do. Dear me, how puzzled I should be if ever I found the smallest difficulty. A penguin that couldn't catch fish would be the funniest thing in the world, *I* think."

"I didn't mean that, Mr. Emperor Penguin," said Tommy Smith. "Only, you see, fishes were made for the water, and they live in it always, and don't have to come out of it for anything. But birds do, of course, to lay their eggs, you know, Mr. Emperor Penguin, and for other things, and a lot of them never go into the water at all, and then most birds fly, and you said that even penguins could fly once, and so they must have gone into the water and got accustomed to it afterwards. But fishes were always there, and don't come on land, so that they're much more accustomed to it, and so it does seem funny that any bird can swim faster than they can in the water, so as to catch them and eat them."

"Well," said the emperor penguin, "I never thought of it like that before. However, it all shows one thing, and that is, how wonderfully clever emperor penguins are. If there *is* any difficulty, that's how I account for it."

"But there are other penguins besides emperor penguins, you know, Mr. Emperor Penguin," said Tommy Smith. "And other birds catch fish in the water as well." (He didn't want him to be *too* conceited.)

"In their case there may be some other reason," said the emperor penguin, after looking puzzled (for the first time) and scratching his head a little, which he did, very cleverly, with one of his big black feet. "But come, let's get on. I don't call this conversation."

"Do you eat anything else besides fish, Mr. Emperor Penguin," asked Tommy Smith.

"Yes, cuttle-fish," said the emperor penguin—plenty of them. And then there are crabs—I like crabs."

"But don't the cuttle-fish catch hold of you with their—with their feelers, Mr. Emperor Penguin?" said Tommy Smith. "And don't the crabs pinch you?"

"I dare say they do, both of them—inside me," said the emperor penguin, "but I don't feel it, and it doesn't last long. You see I only eat small ones, and so can afford to despise their spiteful efforts to injure me."

"Is that all you eat, then, Mr. Emperor Penguin?" said Tommy Smith.

"That and a few stones," said the penguin.

"Stones, Mr. Emperor Penguin," cried Tommy Smith.

"Certainly," said the penguin. "I always like to have a few in my gizzard, because it helps to triturate my food."

"Do you mean to grind it up, Mr. Emperor Penguin?" said Tommy Smith.

"Exactly," said the emperor penguin; "but when there's a choice of words I like to use an elegant one."

Tommy Smith remembered, then, that fowls swallowed stones, just for the very same purpose, and that the wood-pigeon had told him that there was a little mill inside him, by which he meant his gizzard, for that is where the hard things that a bird eats are ground up— the elegant word for which is "triturated." So he wasn't surprised about the penguin's swallowing them, any more. Only, as it was all ice and sea where he lived, he couldn't help asking him where he found these stones.

"At the bottom of the sea when it isn't too deep," said the emperor penguin, "so now you know."

"How do you swim under water, please, Mr. Emperor Penguin?" was the next question that Tommy Smith asked.

"Why, with my paddles, to be sure," the penguin answered, "and so I do above water too. That is to say when I do swim on the top of the sea, but I like going down much better. I can shoot through it ever so much more quickly then. I'd soon show you how, if the sea here were what it ought to be, but it isn't."

"But don't you use your feet, too, Mr. Emperor Penguin?" asked Tommy Smith.

"Yes, to steer with," said the penguin. "I hold them together and stretch them straight out behind me, so that by turning them to this or that side they act like a rudder."

"Oh, I see, like the tail of a fish," said Tommy Smith.

"Like the tail of an emperor penguin," said the emperor penguin.

"I suppose there are a lot of seals where you live, Mr. Emperor Penguin?" said Tommy Smith.

"Oh, ever so many," said the penguin. "There's the waddling seal, as they call him (only they all waddle), and the crab-eating seal, and the sea-lion and sea-elephant, that great mountain of flesh. They're all of them large enough, but he's perfectly enormous. You never saw such a monster, but he's quite loyal and well behaved."

"But aren't they all friendly with you, Mr. Emperor Penguin?" said Tommy Smith.

"Not quite that," said the emperor penguin, drawing himself up a little, though he was very upright before. "I have nothing to complain of in my *subjects,* as a whole. Only the sea-leopard, and he thinks nothing of eating me."

"Oh, that is horrid of him, Mr. Emperor Penguin," said Tommy Smith.

"I can't understand it," said the penguin. "Me—his emperor. It seems very strange, only perhaps he doesn't recognize me in the water—it only happens there. You see I can't walk upright on it as I do on the ice, and so I don't look so imperial. I feel sure that's the reason, for when he sees me on the ice he knows me at once, and he never thinks of eating me then."

"But could he catch you on the ice, Mr. Emperor Penguin?" asked Tommy Smith.

"He might easily when I'm hatching my eggs or rearing my young," said the emperor penguin. "We're in a great crowd then, and we stand only a little higher up on the ice than where the sea-leopards crawl up, out of the sea, to. They might easily get as many of us as they wanted, if they were only to try, for the cliffs are behind us then, and we couldn't all get by them into the sea, and, even if we could, our chicks and eggs would be left. But they never do try because then we look like emperors, and so they know who we are, and that restrains them."

"But then, wouldn't some of the other seals not recog——" Tommy Smith was beginning.

"Anyhow, that's my idea," said the emperor penguin, "and, as I find it a comforting one, I hope you won't try to take it away from me."

So, of course, Tommy Smith couldn't say anything more about it after that, but he didn't think the emperor penguin's idea was a good one.

"Perhaps you would like to know something about our domestic arrangements, now," said the emperor penguin.

"Oh, yes, I should, Mr. Emperor Penguin," said Tommy Smith—for that was just the very thing he had been going to ask about. "You come away from the ice, then, I suppose, and——"

"Come away from it! Why, it's everywhere," said the emperor penguin. "There are some cliffs where some of us go to, but it's all ice where we sit underneath them, and if it wasn't ice it would be the sea. Eggs can't be hatched in the sea, you know."

"But do you lay your eggs on the ice, Mr. Emperor Penguin?" said Tommy Smith.

"My empress lays her egg there," said the emperor penguin. "There is only one egg and one chick. No emperor penguin has more."

This surprised Tommy Smith very much. "Then you've nothing to make a nest with, Mr. Emperor Penguin," he said.

"The ice is our nest," said the emperor penguin. "Except to catch fish for ourselves and our families, we never leave it, from the time when we first lay our egg in the winter till——"

"Don't you mean in the spring, Mr. Emperor Penguin?" said Tommy Smith.

"Certainly not," said the penguin. "We emperor penguins take so long to grow up that, if we laid our eggs in the spring, our little ones would only just be ready to leave us as winter was beginning, and they would not be strong enough to get through it, alone. The storms of wind and snow, which we call blizzards, would kill them. To prevent anything so dreadful, we arrange for them to be little during the winter, and then, when they are the right size to go, it is springtime, and that won't hurt them. Next winter, of course, they will be properly grown."

"It is clever of you to think of it all, Mr. Emperor Penguin," said Tommy Smith.

"Rational foresight, that's all," said the penguin. "And so during the cold dark days of early July——"

"July!" cried Tommy Smith. "Oh, but that's the summer, when it's quite hot. It's midsummer, you know in July, Mr. Emperor Penguin."

"What it may be here, where everything's peculiar," said the emperor penguin, "where there's no proper ice or icebergs, and the sea's not large enough to swim in, I'm sure I don't know. But in my country, where things are not all topsy-turvy, July is midwinter, and that is the time when our empresses feel they have a duty before them, and lay their egg upon the ice."

"But doesn't it get frozen, Mr. Emperor Penguin?" said Tommy Smith.

"It would if we let it stay there too long," said the emperor penguin. "But, as soon as it's laid, we put our feet underneath it, and the soft warm feathers of our body fall down all over it, so that it is quite protected, and the cold can't get to it at all."

"It's clever of you to sit on your egg like that, Mr. Emperor Penguin," said Tommy Smith.

"We don't sit on our egg, we stand on it," said the emperor penguin.

"Stand on it, Mr. Emperor Penguin!" cried Tommy Smith.

"Yes," said the emperor penguin, "only we don't stand *on* it, of course, because that would break it."

"Yes, of course, it would, Mr. Emperor Penguin," said Tommy Smith. "And besides you put your feet under the egg, you know."

"That's right," said the emperor penguin. "No, we don't stand *on* it, of course, only we do stand on it, because we don't sit on it—that is—" The penguin stopped, for a little, looking quite bewildered, and then went on again: "What I mean, only it's rather puzzling, is that we keep standing all the while we're sitting. You understand now, I hope."

"Yes, I think I do, Mr. Emperor Penguin," said Tommy Smith. "Only——"

"Oh, that's enough," said the penguin. "Ask me another question about something else, before my head turns round. It's *the* most puzzling thing that I know."

"But then, how do your feathers fall down over the egg, please, Mr. Emperor Penguin, as you said they did?" asked Tommy Smith. "Because they're not very long, you know."

"They fall down over it because my skin does," the emperor penguin answered. "A little above my feet, just at the right place for it, I have a rather large fold or flap of skin—see here it is (and the penguin showed it), which comes right down over the egg and quite wraps it up. And then, besides that, we lift up our feet—like this, you see, this is the attitude—so as to press the egg close up against its beautiful warm feather-coat. In fact, the egg is in a snug little warm room, and whoever heard of anything getting frozen in a snug little warm room?"

"It is clever of you, Mr. Emperor Penguin," said Tommy Smith, again. "And, of course, when the chick comes out of the egg, it's there too."

"Of course it is," said the emperor penguin. "Where else should it be?—and it stays there as long as it's little enough. Only, of course, from time to time there's a change from one room to another."

"Do you mean that first one of the two penguins takes it and then the other?" asked Tommy Smith.

"Of the two! Of the twenty—or more," said the emperor penguin. "That's what I mean."

Tommy Smith didn't understand this at all. "Of course there's the mother penguin and the father penguin," he was beginning, "but with other birds——"

"I don't know how it may be with other birds," said the emperor penguin, "but every emperor penguin is the child of the penguinary."

"Of the pen-guin-a-ry?" said Tommy Smith. He had never heard such a word before, but, of course, he knew it must have something to do with penguins.

"Certainly," said the emperor penguin. "When an assemblage of penguins is gathered together for a certain purpose, at a certain place, that place is the penguinary. Many quite well-meaning people call it a rookery, but let me tell them that every time they do, they insult penguins, and especially emperor penguins. Rookery indeed! Do they ever call rookeries penguinaries? No. Then where's the justice of it?"

"But do all the penguins at the penguinary take care of the young penguins, Mr. Emperor Penguin?" asked Tommy Smith.

"They do," said the emperor penguin proudly, "and all honour to them for doing so."

"But don't they all have their own young penguin to look after?" said Tommy Smith. And indeed it was a very natural question.

"Oh, no," said the emperor penguin, "because, you see, a great many of our empresses don't lay their egg."

"Oh, but why not, Mr. Emperor Penguin?" said Tommy Smith.

"Imperial caprice—and the climate's so severe," said the emperor penguin hurriedly, and then went on without stopping: "The consequence is, that, round every bird that is either hatching its egg or nursing its young one, there stands a devoted band of friends, both emperors and empresses, determined to help it to do so, and as soon as it goes off to sea, to catch fish, they all make a rush, and fight together to take charge of the precious young life."

"Do they really fight, Mr. Emperor Penguin?" said Tommy Smith.

"How can they help it when all of them want the little thing?" said the emperor penguin. "You see, it's a battle of love for our offspring. Oh, it's a grand sight to see a dozen or twenty fine, splendid emperor penguins, all struggling, in a mass, over one little white fluffy thing that can hardly be seen, in the confusion, all kicking and clawing at each other, and trying to push each other away, until, at last, the strongest wins, and the chick— God bless it!—is tenderly nursed and fostered, until that bird has to leave in its turn. Then, of course, there's the same thing again."

"I wonder the chick isn't hurt, Mr. Emperor Penguin," said Tommy Smith.

"Oh, but it is, very often," said the emperor penguin, "and very often, too, it's killed."

"Killed?" cried Tommy Smith.

"Why, you can see, it can't always be avoided," said the emperor penguin. "You know we're so heavy, we emperor penguins are, seventy or eighty pounds we weigh, and more than that very often. Sometimes one of us will weigh ninety pounds, so that it's really too much for a tender little baby to have first one of us, and then another, standing upon him, and sometimes kicking, and scratching him by mistake. You can't wonder, and, after all, it's all through the tender love we have for him, and our strong wish to help one another."

"Yes, that's all very well, Mr. Emperor Penguin," said Tommy Smith, "but if it kills the chick——" He really felt quite shocked.

"It doesn't always," said the emperor penguin. "You mustn't get exaggerated ideas. And even when it does, there is many and many a one among us who will go on nursing it, all the same."

"Oh, whatever good can that do, Mr. Emperor Penguin?" said Tommy Smith, indignantly. "He isn't alive, and so——"

"No, but he's frozen," said the emperor penguin. "As soon as a chick's dead, he freezes—everything does in our country—and then he can be nursed just the same. Only he won't eat then, poor little thing. That's the worst part of it. Oh dear! He doesn't seem dead, only he won't grow and he refuses his food. And yet we nurse him so. Oh dear!"

"Oh, what *is* the use of nursing him when he's dead, Mr. Emperor Penguin?" said Tommy Smith. He couldn't help speaking impatiently.

"We act for the best," said the poor penguin, looking quite unhappy. "You see it's our way—it's come down to us."

"I think it's a very bad way, Mr. Emperor Penguin," said Tommy Smith. "Why should the poor little penguins be killed by the great big ones fighting for them and hurting them? And what good does it do them to nurse them after they're dead, when they're frozen? I think that's horrid."

"Come, come," said the emperor penguin, "we must remember that nothing is quite perfect in this world, and that some flaw or other can always be discovered if we make up in our minds to find fault. Perhaps we may not do everything quite so well as we might, but we do as well as we can, and we mean still better. Oh, how we do love our little chicks, and how sorry we are when we kill them! But we live in a rough country, and the climate's very much against us."

"How often does the poor little chick get killed, Mr. Emperor Penguin?" asked Tommy Smith.

"Full of snowstorms and blizzards," the emperor penguin went on, without answering; "and the winters are very long, and it's dark all the time, and then fish and crabs and cuttle-fish all have to be caught, whatever the season of the year. And stones must be found, too."

"Yes, Mr. Emperor Penguin," said Tommy Smith. "But do tell——"

"And what with all that," continued the emperor penguin, "and the cliffs under which we sit, with our eggs and our young ones, sometimes breaking and tumbling right down on us, so that quite a lot of us are killed, every winter, and what with sea-leopards and killer-whales—which are worse (I've not told you about them)—eating hundreds and hundreds of us, it's all we can do to keep ourselves alive, very often, and, just as often, we can't."

"It is very dreadful, Mr. Emperor Penguin," said Tommy Smith. "But how often does the little chick get killed? I wish you'd tell me."

"Let me see," said the emperor penguin. "Why, sometimes, out of about eighty, thirty will be brought up and go away with us upon the floating ice, when the sea breaks it off at our penguinaries. But then a good many eggs will not be hatched out as well."

"Only thirty!" cried Tommy Smith. "Then fifty must be killed! Oh, how dreadful, Mr. Emperor Penguin!" It was even worse than he had felt sure it was.

"The climate's so severe," said the emperor penguin.

"It isn't all the climate," said Tommy Smith.

"Of course that's counting the blizzards and the cliffs falling and all the rest that I've told you, and a lot of other things too," said the emperor penguin. "Oh, you don't know what a winter in my country's like. If only you could spend one there and try for yourself—I'd go with you, if you'd take me, of course."

"No, I don't want to go there at all, Mr. Emperor Penguin," said Tommy Smith. "It must be a dreadful country, and I'm sure I shouldn't like it."

"But you like me, don't you?" said the emperor penguin.

"Oh, yes, Mr. Emperor Penguin," said Tommy Smith. Perhaps he wasn't quite so sure as that, but he didn't know what else to say. It was such a funny question.

"Then you mustn't be ungrateful to my country," said the emperor penguin. "Without it you would never have had me, because it's the only country where I'm found."

"Is it, Mr. Emperor Penguin?" said Tommy Smith.

"The only one," said the emperor penguin, "so that if

it had not been there, I should not have been anywhere. Try to think what that means."

Tommy Smith did try, but before he was quite able to, the emperor penguin went on speaking: "Always remember," he said, "and always feel grateful when you do remember, that if it had not been for that country of mine, with its ice and its snow and its cold and its blizzards, and its long winter night, and everything else you think 'dreadful,' there would be no such bird now, in the whole wide world, as—the emperor penguin!"

And when the emperor penguin had said that he made Tommy Smith a still lower bow than any of the other ones he had made him before, and then walked off, in a very stately way, to where the rest of the penguins were standing. Of course Tommy Smith had to bow, too, again, as well as he could, and then he walked off to the elephant.

CHAPTER III

THE AFRICAN ELEPHANT

WHEN Tommy Smith came to the elephant, he looked at him, for some time, without saying anything (only first of all he gave him a bun), thinking what an enormous animal he was. Then he remembered that there are two kinds of elephants, and he wasn't sure which of the two this one was. So he said: "Please, Mr. Elephant, are you the Indian elephant or the African elephant?"

"Oh, I am the African elephant," said the elephant. "You can tell that directly, by my ears. My brother of India has very much smaller ones. Mine are of the full size." And as he said this, the elephant brought both his huge ears forward, so that they stood out on each side of his head, like great flaps (which, indeed, is what they were). As he stood with them like that, he seemed, with his great head between them, to be almost as broad as the whole front of his cage. He might well say that they were of the full size.

"Oh, Mr. Elephant, you have got large ears," cried Tommy Smith. "Why is it that you make them stand out like that, please? Is it to hear better?"

The African Elephant

"That's one of the reasons," said the elephant. "Pigmy animals use them in that way too. Besides that, it helps to frighten my enemies when they provoke me to rush at them, and then, too, I flap myself with my ears—in this way—I'm very fond of doing that."

"What do you do it for, Mr. Elephant?" asked Tommy Smith.

"Oh, to get rid of the flies and the dust," said the elephant; "but, besides that, it's a very pleasant thing in itself. As for hearing, perhaps it makes me hear just a little better when I spread my ears out like that."

"But you hear quite well, anyhow, don't you, Mr. Elephant?" said Tommy Smith. He felt very surprised indeed that he should speak as if he didn't.

"Well enough, well enough, I dare say," said the

elephant. "If it were necessary for me to hear better, no doubt I should. But hearing is not the sense that I most rely on."

"Then I suppose you see very well, Mr. Elephant," said Tommy Smith. Of course he was still more surprised now, because he had always thought that the larger an animal's ears were the better it must hear, and the elephant's, he felt sure, were the largest of all, even for such a large animal. He was not quite right about that, but that was what he thought.

"As well as I can be expected to," the elephant answered. "My own people, and anyone else not quite dwarfish, I can see just as well as you see me. But, you see, the world is full of pigmies, and when one of the kind you belong to comes creeping up to me amongst the trees and bushes where I am standing, hiding himself behind first one and then another of them (as if he were not small enough without that), why, then, of course, I often don't see him. That makes him think my eyesight is bad, and he tells other people that it is, and so it gets into the natural history books."

"I didn't know that anybody said you couldn't see well, Mr. Elephant," said Tommy Smith.

"The pigmies that shoot at me do," said the elephant, "but I dare say if a lizard or a fly or a beetle were to come up to them through the forest, and were to keep hiding itself all the time, they wouldn't see it always, either. Those little murderous dwarfs ought to consider how easy it must be for a properly grown animal, like an elephant, not to notice them, even when they are crawling and creeping in full view. For my part, when I'm not thinking of a pigmy, I hardly notice him even when I do see him, and one can't always be thinking of him because he's always wanting to murder one. However, my eyesight, good as it is—it would be quite good enough, I'm sure, in a peaceable world—is not the sense I most rely on."

Tommy Smith couldn't help wondering which of his five senses the elephant did most rely on, if it was neither sight nor hearing, for he had always thought that those were the two most important ones. The best way of finding out was to ask him, so he said: "Please, Mr. Elephant, which of your senses is it that you do most rely on?"

"Why, scent, to be sure," said the elephant.

"Scent, Mr. Elephant?" said Tommy Smith.

"Oh, but is that really more useful to you than seeing and hearing?"

"When I'm in danger it is," said the elephant, "and I think that makes it the most useful. As long as the wind is blowing in the right direction—by which I mean from him to me—it doesn't matter at all whether I can see or hear a pigmy, because I can always smell him—he has such a strong and unpleasant scent."

"I suppose you mean that all animals have, Mr. Elephant," said Tommy Smith, "because you call them all pigmies, but——"

"So they are," said the elephant, "all except the rhinoceros and hippopotamus, who are undersized merely, and the giraffe, who is certainly tall, but too thin. Why there should be so many pigmies in the world I'm sure I don't know, but so it is. As you say, they all have a strong scent, but perhaps that's because my own sense of smell is so strong. But the man-pigmy, which was the one I was thinking most about, has not only a very strong scent, but a very unpleasant one too."

Tommy Smith didn't like this idea at all, because, of course, he was a man-pigmy (or a little boy-pigmy) himself. At any rate, that was what the elephant called him, so he said: "I don't see why, Mr. Elephant."

"It's because *he's* so unpleasant," said the elephant.

Tommy Smith thought this was an even more disagreeable remark of the elephant's than the last one, and the two together made him feel very uncomfortable. He wanted to make some good answer, but he couldn't think of anything better than just to say: "Oh no, Mr. Elephant, not all of them, you know."

"I'm only talking of the ones that come to murder me," said the elephant. "They are most unpleasant, so I think the two things must go together. When a man-pigmy only comes to look at me, I can put up with him, and then I put up with his scent as well."

Tommy Smith thought it was best to go on to something else, so he said: "I suppose it's with your trunk that you smell, Mr. Elephant, because, of course, your trunk is your nose."

"It's several things, all together," said the elephant. "It's a nose and a hand and arm, and a snake, and a syringe, because, you know, I can squirt water, with it, over myself or anybody else, when I want to."

"Yes, I know you can, Mr. Elephant, and I'd like to see you do it—over yourself," said Tommy Smith.

"There's no water here, or else I'd show you," said the elephant—and Tommy Smith was rather glad of this, in case it might have been over himself.

"I suppose you mean your trunk's a snake because you can twist it round things, Mr. Elephant," said Tommy Smith.

"Of course," said the elephant—"like this." And he began twisting his trunk round the thick wooden bars of his cage, first the ones that were fixed in the ground, and then the one at the top that ran across them, and that their ends were fixed into. "What else is there except a snake that could do that?" he asked. "Your arm could not, because it has joints in it, so that it always has to be stiff except just where you bend it, which is only in one or two places. It must be a great inconvenience to you to have an arm that is stiff in most parts of it, so that you can never twist it round anything, like a snake, as I can twist my arm. No other animal, except an elephant, can do that."

"But then no other animal has a trunk, you know, Mr. Elephant," said Tommy Smith. "But some animals can do it with their tails. There's the o———"

"*I* should consider that vulgar," said the elephant, "so we won't talk of it. And then at the end of *my* arm," he continued, "I have a hand with a finger and thumb (which is all one wants), as you must have noticed just now when I took the bun you were so kind as to give me. And that hand and long arm of mine that bends everywhere, is a nose as well; so you see what a wonderful thing my trunk is."

"Yes, Mr. Elephant," said Tommy Smith (he quite agreed with him), "but I suppose your trunk is more a nose than a hand and arm."

The elephant did not answer directly, but stood silently swaying his head from one side to another, in a slow sort of way, as if he were considering. At last he said: "When I am smelling with it more than I am picking leaves off the branches of trees, or twisting it round grass to pull it out of the ground, then it is more a nose than a hand and arm, but when I am doing that or other things like that, more than I am smelling with it, then it is more a hand and arm than a nose. And when it's only doing one or the other, or not doing anything, then——"

"Yes, Mr. Elephant," said Tommy Smith. But instead of finishing the sentence, the elephant only said, after making another long pause and swinging his head again: "Anyhow it's more important for me as a hand even than as a nose, because if I couldn't use it as a hand, I should not be able to eat, which, of course, is more important than smelling or anything, even than killing my enemies."

"But you do that with your tusks, don't you, Mr. Elephant?" said Tommy Smith.

"I do it just as much with my trunk," said the elephant,

"and it is because of my trunk that I am able to catch my enemies without even seeing them, sometimes."

"Without seeing them, Mr. Elephant!" cried Tommy Smith, for he couldn't understand that at all.

"You see," said the elephant, "my enemies are almost always the man-pigmies, and a man-pigmy is so small, and there are so many bushes and trees in the way, that often I can't see him, even when I'm running after him."

"But you see him before you catch him, don't you, Mr. Elephant?" said Tommy Smith.

"Not always," said the elephant. "Sometimes I should run right over him, without seeing him, if it were not for my trunk. But my trunk keeps on smelling him, till, at last, it touches him, and as soon as it touches him, I catch him with it."

"What do you do with him after you've caught him, Mr. Elephant?" asked Tommy Smith.

"Put him under my feet and stamp on him," answered the elephant, "or sometimes I kneel on him, and kill him in that way. A touch almost kills him, because he's only a poor, wretched, weak little creature, but the worst of it is that he's so small that often he gets away, even from right under my feet, before I quite know where he is. I remember once catching one of the black man-pigmies that swarm so in my country, who got away like that three times, and the third time I couldn't catch him again."

"Do tell me about it, please, Mr. Elephant," said Tommy Smith.

"Oh, there's not much to tell," said the elephant. "Although he was only a black man he had a gun, and shot me with it, but the wound was not a bad one, though it hurt me very much and made me very angry. I got his scent and ran right down on him, and caught him and laid him on the ground, between my feet, on his back. Then I lifted up one of my great feet, as you would call them, because yours are so small, and stamped down with it upon him, or, at least, that was what I meant to do. But as it came down, he threw himself over to the other side, against my other foot, so that instead of coming down right upon him, it only just grazed his side. Then when I lifted my other foot up, he rolled over the opposite way, so that I missed him with that one too, and when that had gone on for some time he managed to get away, and crawl out between my hind legs, and run off. I turned round and ran after him and caught him again, but he got away again in just the same way, and so he did even a third time, so that I think he must have had a charmed life."

"Did you catch him again after that, Mr. Elephant?" asked Tommy Smith.

"No—not again," said the elephant. "I was unlucky with that man-pigmy, and lost him. But I didn't lose another that I caught some time afterwards."

"Why didn't you, Mr. Elephant?" asked Tommy Smith.

"Oh, I kept him in my trunk the whole time," said the elephant, "and put one foot on him very carefully, and pulled him in half."

"Oh, how dreadful, Mr. Elephant!" said Tommy Smith.

"After that there was no more difficulty," the elephant continued, "so I pulled off one of his legs, and then left him."

"Oh, Mr. Elephant, how dreadful!" said Tommy Smith again. "But of course he had fired at you first, and wounded you."

"Of course he had," said the elephant. "He had meant to kill me and as many other elephants as he could. I had cows and young calves to defend."

"Yes, Mr. Elephant," said Tommy Smith. He knew that by cows he meant female elephants, and that the calves were the young elephants.

"You don't blame me, I hope?" said the elephant.

"No, it wasn't your fault, Mr. Elephant," said Tommy Smith. But still what the elephant had told him made him feel very uncomfortable, and as he looked up at the great animal before him, and thought how terribly strong he was, and what dreadful things he could do, he could not help stepping back a little from the barrier in front of his cage, as if he thought his trunk was long enough to reach to where he was.

Perhaps the elephant guessed what he was feeling, for he looked rather hurt, and said: "I never do things like that here, where I am properly treated. You know I come out of my house upon fine summer days and walk all about the Gardens without hurting anyone. Instead of hurting people, I give them rides on my back. That is because they treat me well here and give me buns, but in the country where I live, man-pigmies are very dangerous, and I don't really know which are the worst, the white or the black ones."

"Aren't the white men the most dangerous, Mr. Elephant?" said Tommy Smith (*he* wasn't going to say "pigmies"), "because they always have guns, you know, and sometimes black people haven't—and they can shoot better than black men can, too."

"As for that," said the elephant, "I call a pigmy dangerous when he can kill me in any way, and sometimes the least painful way is to be shot. In some parts of Africa there are man-pigmies who ride upon other pigmy animals, not quite so small as they are, called horses. They kill us with swords, and don't——"

"With swords, Mr. Elephant?" cried Tommy Smith, for it seemed to him quite impossible that a great elephant should be killed in such a way as that.

"Yes, with swords," said the elephant, "and really I think that is the worst way of all. At any rate it is the longest, because we have to bleed to death."

"Please tell me about it, Mr. Elephant," said Tommy Smith.

"The man-pigmies who kill us in that way," said the elephant, "are very great riders. They are not like the other ones that molest us, either the whites or the tall black or brown ones, with black curly hair that grows close to their heads, or the light yellow ones that are in two sizes, one almost as tall as the black kind, and the other only about half their height, and so little that I class them as insects."

"Oh, those are the Bushmen, Mr. Elephant," said Tommy Smith, "only they're bigger than that, and just as much men as the other ones are."

"A sort of large insect they look like," said the elephant. "But they are men, I know, and we call them the pigmy man-pigmies. Some of them are brown, too, like the bigger kinds, and those, I think, are the smallest of all, only I should have to hold one of each close together, to make quite sure which of them was. All these pests hunt us on foot, with spears and bows and arrows, or dig pits for us to fall into, or hang iron spikes in the trees, to fall down on our backs and run into us. But those others, who call themselves Arabs, ride after us on their horses, and they have just one sword, with which they strike at our legs and cut the sinews, so that we can't run any more, but have to fall down and bleed to death. They are the worst pests of all, because their horses go so fast that we can't get away from them. Yellow men they are, too, but tall, and with long black hair that hangs down, all round their heads, in long curls."

"But, Mr. Elephant, they must come quite close to you, to use their swords," said Tommy Smith.

"So they do, of course," said the elephant.

"But then, why don't you catch them, Mr. Elephant?" asked Tommy Smith.

"You see, they come behind me, so that I have to

turn round," said the elephant, "but they're so quick that, before I can, they manage to get out of the way."

"I suppose you don't see them coming, Mr. Elephant?" said Tommy Smith, "because, if you did, then you could turn round directly, and wait for them, and they wouldn't come then."

"You don't understand it at all," said the elephant. "I see them coming well enough, because it's open country where these pigmies hunt me. They can't ride amongst bushes, so they wait till they see me away from them. So, of course, I keep looking about, and if they came one at a time, they'd never get near me. But two of them attack me together, and the way they do it is this. One rides right in front of me, so near that he seems almost under my trunk, which, of course, makes me very angry, and I try all I can to catch him. But however fast I go, that horrid little creature of a horse, who, of course, is trained to do it, keeps just out of my reach, and whilst I am trying to get hold of him or of the man upon him, with my trunk, and can't think of anything else, the other pigmy rides his horse almost underneath me, and then jumps off it as quickly as if he were a monkey, and, as I sweep by, he makes a dreadful slash at my hind-leg that is nearest to him, just above the foot, and that cuts the sinews, so that I can't run any more, but have to stop. Then the pigmy in front of me stops his horse too, and they turn round, together, and face me. The man-pigmy bends down to the ground and picks up some sand or dirt, which he throws at me—right in my face. Of course I am enraged at such an insult, and try to rush at him, but I can only go quite slowly however much I try, and, as he rides off again, the other one gallops up on the other side, and jumps off his horse and slashes at my other leg, this time and then I can't even walk. I have to fall down on the ground and bleed to death as I told you. Perhaps you understand it better now."

"Oh, yes, I do, Mr. Elephant," said Tommy Smith, "and I think it's very cruel of those people to kill you in that way."

"I think it's cruel to kill me in any way," said the elephant.

"Yes, it is, Mr. Elephant," said Tommy Smith. "I suppose it's to get your tusks that they do it."

"My tusks?" said the elephant. "Why, whatever good can they do them?"

"Oh, they're ivory, you know, Mr. Elephant," said Tommy Smith, "and they make a lot of things out of them. They're useful for all sorts of things."

"They're ever so much more useful to me," said the elephant. "It's the most selfish thing I've ever heard of. How would they like to be killed for their teeth, I should like to know."

"No, of course they wouldn't, Mr. Elephant," said Tommy Smith. "But their teeth are only useful to themselves, you know."

"Do you think that's why they wouldn't like it?" said the elephant.

"I know it's not right, Mr. Elephant," said Tommy Smith.

"Right!" said the elephant. "If it's not the most wrong thing there is, then the world must be a very wrong place. That's what I think."

"But you catch the Arabs, too, sometimes, don't you, Mr. Elephant?" said Tommy Smith.

"Not very often," said the elephant, in a sad tone of voice. "They're so active, and I get so confused with their coming behind me and in front of me at the same time. Sometimes four of them will attack me on foot, without horses at all, and yet I can't catch them, because I have to keep turning round every minute, to prevent my hind-legs being slashed at—and yet I can't prevent it for long, unless I can get to the bushes. Only those cunning little pigmies wait till I've got right away from them."

"Don't you ever use your tusks against them and the other men who hunt you, Mr. Elephant?" said Tommy Smith.

"I do when I can, of course," said the elephant, "only it's difficult with pigmies, because they're so small. Once I remember doing it with a white man-pigmy, but that was only after trying several times. At first I kept missing, and then I only hit him on the head with one, and it was only one that went through him, at last, after all. I had to stamp him under my feet, to make quite sure that he was dead."

"I'm sure he must have been dead, Mr. Elephant," said Tommy Smith. He thought it was dreadfully savage.

"I was, too, then," said the elephant, "but it took me some time to be. No, tusks are awkward for pigmies."

"But what do you use your tusks for most, Mr. Elephant?" asked Tommy Smith.

"For fighting and eating," said the elephant. "When two of us male elephants have a fight, we try all we can to drive our tusks into each other, and the one who can do that first generally wins—at least if he can do it properly. Then for eating" (Tommy Smith had been wondering how the elephant could use them in that way), "we tear off the bark of the trees with them, and the bark of trees is one of the principal things that we live on."

"I thought it was the leaves of trees, Mr. Elephant," said Tommy Smith.

"I said one of the principal things," said the elephant. "The leaves of trees is another. Then we like some things that grow underground too, and sometimes we dig those up with our tusks and sometimes we stamp holes in the ground with our feet, and pull them out of the holes with our trunks."

"I suppose no animal ever attacks you, Mr. Elephant," said Tommy Smith, "because you're so much larger and stronger than any other animal."

"Of course there's the lion-pigmy," said the elephant. "He does annoy me sometimes, before I'm grown up."

"When you're quite young, I suppose you mean, Mr. Elephant," said Tommy Smith.

"Oh, yes," said the elephant, "not more than ten or twelve years old, perhaps."

"Oh, but does it take you so long as that to grow up,

Mr. Elephant?" said Tommy Smith. He knew that most animals grow up very much more quickly than men do.

"It takes me thirty-five years to do it properly," said the elephant, "and sometimes I live till I'm a hundred and fifty years old."

"Oh, Mr. Elephant, that is a long time," said Tommy Smith.

"It's not too long for me," said the elephant. "I hope when you're only half as old you'll be able to say the same."

"Do you fight lions when they attack you, Mr. Elephant?" asked Tommy Smith. He couldn't think of anything to say to his last remark, so he didn't say anything.

"Of course at that early age I should not have much chance with one," said the elephant. "But it's very seldom that I'm attacked, even then, because I keep with the herd, and no lion would come amongst a herd of elephants if he could help it."

"Would you all attack him, Mr. Elephant?" said Tommy Smith.

"I should think we would," said the elephant, "especially if he were to try to interfere with any of the young ones belonging to the herd. Supposing just one of us were to see him creeping up through the bushes, he would throw up his trunk and trumpet—like this." (The elephant threw up his trunk and trumpeted so loudly and shrilly, it seemed to go right through Tommy Smith.) Then every other elephant that heard him, and saw or guessed what it was about, would trumpet too, and we would all rush down together on that brigand, for the ones that saw him would lead the others. That is how we grown-up elephants protect our young ones from lions."

"It's very good of you, Mr. Elephant," said Tommy Smith.

"That's not all we do to help each other," said the elephant. "If one of us is wounded and gets away, but can't get any farther, and there is no water where he is, then some of his friends will bring him water, in the night."

"Oh, just fancy, Mr. Elephant!" said Tommy Smith. "But then, how do you carry it?"

"Why, inside us, of course," said the elephant. "We drink it ourselves first, and then we draw it up into our trunks again, and squirt it into the mouth of the poor wounded one."

"Oh, it is good of you, Mr. Elephant," said Tommy Smith.

"Elephants must help one another," said the elephant, "and it is the duty of every member of the herd to look after its young ones. Ah, how happy I was when I was a baby elephant!"

"You were quite little then, Mr. Elephant, I suppose," said Tommy Smith.

"I was a pigmy, like you," said the elephant, "but I never seemed to myself to be one. All around me in the forests, amongst the great trees under whose shadow

I was born, stood tall, grey, stately forms, like me, but much larger, and I always felt, when I looked up at them, that some day I should be as large and tall and stately as they were. It made me feel happy to be amongst them, and as I grew up from day to day, and went striding through the forests with my great companions, plucking the green tender leaves and pulling up great sheathes of the juicy luscious grasses, to chew into pulp when I was hungry: drinking the beautiful, cool, liquid water when I was thirsty: bathing and rolling in it, and spouting it over my back and sides when I was hot, and it was pleasant to do that: feeling the warm sun upon me in the fresh early morning: standing and sleeping in the cool shade when it was too hot to——"

"Oh, but do you sleep standing up, Mr. Elephant?" said Tommy Smith.

"Almost always," said the elephant. "But I hadn't quite finished my sentence."

"Oh, do finish it, please, Mr. Elephant," said Tommy Smith.

"It isn't so easy now," said the elephant. "Puffing the dust over my back was coming, and having a mud-bath and a lot of other things. What I mean is, that doing all those delightful things every day, and not having anything to worry or annoy me, and getting bigger and stronger and handsomer as time went on, I used to think no life could be happier than the life of an elephant. And then, all at once, came the man-pigmy."

"And the lion-pigmy, too, you know, Mr. Elephant," said Tommy Smith.

"Pshaw!" said the elephant (at least he made a noise with his trunk that sounded very like that), "he's not worth considering. It would be an accident even if he were to kill a baby elephant. After we're babies, we soon grow too big and too strong for him."

"Oh, yes, Mr. Elephant," said Tommy Smith—for it was just what he had thought.

"We bulls, at any rate," said the elephant. "It does sometimes happen that when lions are very hungry and have not been able to get pigmy-meat, five or six of them together will attack a cow-elephant, and even kill her and eat her."

"Will they really, Mr. Elephant?" said Tommy Smith.

"It has been known," said the elephant, "but, of course, it is a very rare thing."

"But was the cow-elephant grown up, Mr. Elephant?" asked Tommy Smith.

"Very nearly, if not quite," said the elephant.

"But then, couldn't a lot of lions kill a full-grown bull-elephant too, Mr. Elephant?" said Tommy Smith.

"Never!" said the elephant—and again he threw up his trunk, and gave a shrill and very loud trumpet. "Even twenty of them together would not dare to attempt it, and lions don't hunt in packs. If they did, and if the whole pack of them attacked me, I would think no more of them than if they were so many ants." (Tommy Smith couldn't help thinking that this was boasting, even in an elephant.) "No, no, there is only one kind of pigmy-animal that a full-grown bull-elephant need feel in the least alarmed about."

"I suppose you mean men, Mr. Elephant," said Tommy Smith, though he didn't think that men were animals.

"I'm obliged to mean them," said the elephant, severely, "but I'm only talking of grown-up ones, and I've nothing to say against any man-pigmy who comes here and gives me a bun."

"The elephant made a sort of salaam as he said this, by lifting his head and sinking it down again, a little lower than usual. Tommy Smith thought it was his way of saying good-bye, because, after he had done it, he walked to the back of his cage, and stood there, without saying anything more.

So Tommy Smith thought that he had better say good-bye as well, and when he had said it, in his way, he went off to see some other animal. But what animal was it going to be? The rhinoceros was in the very same "house" as the elephant, and the hippopotamus' "house" was only a little way further on, and they were both very interesting animals. But Tommy Smith felt even more interested in the grizzly bear, and so, as it was impossible to talk to all the animals that he wanted to talk to, on the same day, because there were so many of them, he made up his mind that his next conversation should be with him.

CHAPTER IV

THE GRIZZLY BEAR

THE great grizzly bear looked so grim and so grizzly when Tommy Smith came up—not to the bars of his cage, because no one was allowed to do that, but to a paling in front of them, which prevented one's coming too near—that he felt quite nervous about beginning the conversation—for the grizzly bear didn't help him. But at last he said: "Well, Mr. Grizzly Bear."

"Well," said the grizzly bear. It was a gruff voice, but it did not sound ill-tempered.

"You're a very fierce animal, aren't you, Mr. Grizzly Bear?" said Tommy Smith, for he had always heard that, and it was in good natural history books too.

"Explain yourself," said the grizzly bear.

"Oh, I mean you're very dangerous, aren't you, Mr. Grizzly Bear?" said Tommy Smith, "because, you know, when you see a man you don't run away, but always attack him directly, and——"

"You've got it the wrong way," said the grizzly bear. "Directly I see a man I run away as fast as I can, but *he* attacks *me,* as soon as he sees me."

The Grizzly Bear

"But *then,* you're very dangerous, aren't you, Mr. Grizzly Bear?" said Tommy Smith.

"He is," said the grizzly bear. "You've got it the wrong way again." Tommy Smith was very surprised indeed to hear the grizzly bear talk in this way, because it was so different from what the natural history books said. "Why do you run away from a man, when you see him, Mr. Grizzly Bear?" he asked.

"Because, if I don't, he kills me with thunderbolts," the grizzly bear answered.

"With thunderbolts, Mr. Grizzly Bear?" said Tommy Smith, for at first he didn't understand what the grizzly bear meant.

"Yes, it's always in that way now," the grizzly bear answered. "Even though I do run away, he generally kills me with them, so that, if I didn't, he'd be sure to."

"Don't you meant that he shoots you, Mr. Grizzly Bear?" said Tommy Smith.

"Perhaps I do," said the grizzly bear, "but it's with thunderbolts."

"Oh, no, Mr. Grizzly Bear," said Tommy Smith. "It's with a gun he shoots you, and he fires bullets out of it. They're not thunderbolts."

"Well, I don't understand them," said the grizzly bear, "but whatever they are, they hit me from a long way off, when there's nobody near me that I can hit back at, and they make a great noise and smoke, and there's a flash sometimes, and they've a disagreeable smell, too, which is what I call being a thunderbolt. Why, I remember once there were five of us on a hill—one a poor mother, with two cubs—all feeding peacefully, when five claps of thunder came, one after another, and there we all lay dead. What could have done that except thunderbolts?—and don't you think it was a very wicked thing to hit us with them, and kill us?"

"Yes, I do, Mr. Grizzly Bear," said Tommy Smith (he saw it was no use trying to explain to him that guns were not thunderbolts). "I think it's very wicked to kill animals when they don't attack people, and don't do any harm."

"Even if they did do a little harm, I don't think they ought to be killed for it," said the grizzly bear. "I call that too severe. Would you like to be punished in that way?"

"Oh, no, Mr. Grizzly Bear," said Tommy Smith.

"I suppose you do a little harm sometimes?" said the grizzly bear.

"Yes, perhaps I do—a little, Mr. Grizzly Bear," said Tommy Smith.

"We weren't doing any," said the grizzly bear, "only just eating our dinners, which were of roots and berries. Five quite innocent bears we were, but five thunderbolts came, and there we all lay dead upon the hillside."

"I think it was dreadful, Mr. Grizzly Bear," said Tommy Smith.

"When a man can do that," said the grizzly bear, "he's dangerous to us, and it's no use pretending that we're dangerous to him. We used to be once, but now we're not any longer. He understands thunderbolts and we don't."

"Oh, then you were a dangerous animal once, Mr. Grizzly Bear," said Tommy Smith. He was very glad indeed to hear that.

"Yes, once I was," said the grizzly bear, "but I'm not now at all."

"But why have you changed, Mr. Grizzly Bear?" said Tommy Smith.

"Oh, you see, it was all different then," said the grizzly bear. "Those were the good old times, before thunderbolts. Thunderbolts had not come into the country then, and even for a long time after they did come into it, they were not nearly such bad ones as they are now. They were not bad enough for me to be afraid of, and, of course, as long as I was not afraid of thunderbolts I was not afraid of men. Why should I have been? A man without thunderbolts was a much weaker being than myself. I was not afraid when I got his scent or came upon his tracks, and if I met him I never thought of running away from him."

"Did he run away from you when he met you, Mr. Grizzly Bear?" asked Tommy Smith.

"Not if he was a wise man," the grizzly bear answered. "If it was an Indian, and he didn't want to fight me, he would stand still and look at me, and after I had looked at him, a little, I just walked on, and there was an end of it. When the white men first came into the country they didn't understand me so well, and sometimes they would run away from me, and then sometimes I would run after them. But it was only curiosity that made me do that. You see, they were a different sort of people to any that I'd seen before. Neither their scent nor their colour was like that of the Indians, and they did not dress in the same way. It was natural I should want to look at them."

"Weren't they very frightened when you ran after them, Mr. Grizzly Bear?" said Tommy Smith.

"Very," said the grizzly bear, "but that generally made them do something that made me run away myself."

"Oh, then you were frightened too, even then, Mr. Grizzly Bear," said Tommy Smith.

"No, not frightened, only startled," said the grizzly bear. "We only got frightened of white people when we found out they could kill us, and knew they always wanted to kill us. Before that, they only startled us sometimes with their odd ways and appearance. They were new to us, but though we thought them funny and not nearly so nice-looking as the Indians, still we had quite friendly feelings towards them, only they wouldn't understand that. I remember once following one of them in a quite friendly way till he actually ran into a river, and then he turned round, all of a sudden, and pushed something at me quite rudely, and then I turned round too, and off I went. I wasn't frightened but it surprised me, and I couldn't help feeling a little hurt."

"What did he push at you, Mr. Grizzly Bear?" asked Tommy Smith.

"Oh, something so curious," said the grizzly bear. "I think it must have been a thunderbolt, because it felt hard and flashed like the sun. But there was no noise, and it didn't hurt me, so if it was, it was a weak one. Thunderbolts then were not what they are now."

"It was his gun, I think, Mr. Grizzly Bear," said Tommy Smith, "only it wasn't loaded. The sun made it flash, perhaps. It wasn't a real flash, you know, because then it would have made a great bang."

"Whatever it was, I didn't like it," said the grizzly bear. "It was an awkward incident, but nothing serious happened."

"Yes, that's all very well, Mr. Grizzly Bear," said Tommy Smith, "but it wasn't very nice for the man you ran after to have to go into a river and get wet."

"I didn't mean him to," said the grizzly bear, "and it was only up to his waist."

"Only, indeed! Mr. Grizzly Bear," said Tommy Smith, "I call that quite deep enough, and I don't wonder people were frightened of you, if you used to run after them and drive them into rivers."

"They didn't understand me," said the grizzly bear, "and that made them nervous, and when people are nervous they act foolishly. But there was one white man who did understand me, and, because he did, he was not nervous about me at all. He used to go about looking for berries or digging in the ground for roots, which, of course, I could quite understand. I used to come and look at him and say to myself, 'One of them's sensible, at any rate!' He didn't seem to mind me at all, only when I came rather too near, as he thought, he used just to shake something that made a queer rattling noise, as if it had pebbles inside it."

"I suppose it was a box, then, Mr. Grizzly Bear," said Tommy Smith.

"Very likely," said the grizzly bear, "and then I would

go away. I suppose he thought I wanted to take some of his roots or berries, but that was not my idea at all. There was plenty for both of us, and the plants he took off with him were not what I like."

"Perhaps he was picking flowers, Mr. Grizzly Bear," said Tommy Smith. "But then, it wasn't to eat them, but only to keep them, and look at them, and show them to people, you know."

"Ah, well, I thought he was sensible," said the grizzly bear, "but even if he was not, still he was not rude. He never poked anything at me, but only made that queer sort of noise which I thought meant, 'These roots and berries are mine, and not yours, because I found them.' That was quite right, of course, and I just went off about my own business, in a quite friendly way."

"I think he was a very brave man, Mr. Grizzly Bear," said Tommy Smith.

"He wasn't a nervous man, and he knew I was harmless, that was all," said the grizzly bear. "He was sensible. As for his being brave, all the brave men I have known have been Indians."

"Have they, Mr. Grizzly Bear?" said Tommy Smith.

"Yes," said the grizzly bear, "because when they wanted to have a fight with me they came close up where I could see them, and shot me with their bows and arrows. Of course, that was treating me very badly, but still it was a brave thing to do, because, you see, I am not easy to kill with one arrow, and before the Indian could fire another I was upon him, and then he had only his knife and his tomahawk against these teeth and these claws of mine." The grizzly bear pointed to first one and then the other as he said this, and Tommy Smith agreed that the Indian was a very brave man indeed.

"And then, did you kill him, Mr. Grizzly Bear?" he said.

"When I got the best of it, I did," said the grizzly bear.

"I suppose you gave him a hug, to kill him, Mr. Grizzly Bear?" said Tommy Smith.

"A hug? No," said the grizzly bear, "I gave him a cuff."

"Oh, but didn't you hug him, as well, Mr. Grizzly Bear?" said Tommy Smith.

"Of course not," said the grizzly bear. "Why, we were enemies."

"Oh, yes, of course, Mr. Grizzly Bear," said Tommy Smith. "Only I thought bears always hugged people when they wanted to kill them."

"Grizzly bears don't," said the grizzly bear. "We're not such hypocrites."

"But don't other bears then, Mr. Grizzly Bear?" asked Tommy Smith.

"I should be sorry to think so," said the grizzly bear. "They have their faults—they're not perfect. Oh dear, no—we grizzlies are not, either—but I don't suspect them of that. What!—hug people that you're trying to kill—kill them *by* hugging them! Oh, what shocking hypocrisy!"

"Oh, but not if it was a fight, you know, Mr. Grizzly Bear," said Tommy Smith, "and I thought that bears always hugged people to death."

"Shocking—shocking," said the grizzly bear. "But I hope you'll think better of us in future."

"I didn't think it was like what you mean, Mr. Grizzly Bear," said Tommy Smith. "But how did you kill the Indian, then?"

"Why, with my teeth and claws, to be sure—like other animals—if I did kill him," the grizzly bear answered.

"Oh, but you did generally, didn't you, Mr. Grizzly Bear?" said Tommy Smith.

"It was a fight to the death," said the grizzly bear. "If I killed him, I ate him. If he killed me, he had my skin for a robe, and my claws and teeth to make into a necklace, to wear. Everybody who saw him with that robe or that necklace knew that he was one of the bravest men of the tribe, for it was only by being very brave and very skilful, too, that a poor, feeble, stunted man could have killed me, the great Mishe-Mokwa of the mountains—that was what the Indians called me—with only his bow and arrows, and his knife or tomahawk."

"But aren't the Indians strong men, Mr. Grizzly Bear?" said Tommy Smith, "and aren't they tall, too?"

"Oh, for men they are," said the grizzly bear. "They are often very fine *men* indeed, but they'd be very poor bears. Compared with me, all men are feeble and stunted."

"Oh, yes, I see what you mean now, Mr. Grizzly Bear," said Tommy Smith, "and, of course, it was very brave indeed of the Indian."

"*He* really did face me," said the grizzly bear. "Of course, one can't be expected to like a man who kills one, but still I couldn't help respecting him, because he did it in such a brave way. Besides, he was always very polite to me after he had killed me."

"Oh, but how, Mr. Grizzly Bear?" said Tommy Smith. He thought that a very funny way of being polite to anybody.

"Why, he used to fill his pipe with tobacco, and blow the smoke of it up my nostrils," said the grizzly bear. "That was as much as to beg my pardon for what he had done, and to ask me not to haunt him for doing it."

"Oh, what *do* you mean, Mr. Grizzly Bear?" said Tommy Smith.

"It was his idea," said the grizzly bear. "He thought that unless he was polite to me, like that, my ghost would haunt him, because he had killed me."

"Oh, but that was all nonsense, you know, Mr. Grizzly Bear," said Tommy Smith.

"Anyhow, it's what he always did," said the grizzly bear, "and my ghost never did haunt him—so perhaps there was something in it."

Of course, Tommy Smith knew quite well that there was nothing in it, and that it would have been just the same although the Indian had not blown tobacco smoke up the grizzly bear's nostrils. But he did not say so, because perhaps the grizzly bear would not have believed him and then it would have been so difficult to prove. Besides, he thought that there had been enough about men, now, and he wanted to hear something about the grizzly bear's habits with other animals, because he felt sure that some of these would be interesting. He knew that there were buffaloes in America (though here we called them bisons) as well as in Africa, and if the lion killed buffaloes, to eat them, he thought the grizzly bear, who was much larger and stronger than a lion—though perhaps not so fierce— would be quite able to kill them, too, if he wanted to. And if he ate meat, he would want to, and as he ate Indians, when he did kill them, that showed he did eat meat, and—but, of course, the best way was to ask, so he said: "Please, Mr. Grizzly Bear, do you kill bisons in your country?"

"I used to kill *buffaloes* when they *were* in my country," said the grizzly bear. "But the white men have killed so many of them with their thunderbolts, that now there are very few left."

"But I thought there were such a lot of them, Mr. Grizzly Bear," said Tommy Smith.

"So there were—millions," said the grizzly bear, "and as long as only I and the Indians lived with them, they were always enough for both of us. But they were not enough for the white men, and there are very few left now."

"Oh, but what a pity, Mr. Grizzly Bear," said Tommy Smith.

"It has been the same with all the other animals, and with the Indians as well," said the grizzly bear.

"So now, if you want to know, you musn't ask me how I kill the buffalo, but how I used to kill him when there were enough buffaloes for grizzly bears to kill, and enough grizzly bears to kill buffaloes."

"Oh, I do want to know very much, Mr. Grizzly Bear," said Tommy Smith, "so please tell me how you used to kill the buffalo." Of course he felt very sorry that he had to ask the question in that way.

"First I had to catch him," said the grizzly bear, "and I had one very clever way of doing that. It was not always necessary. Sometimes I could stalk him and take him quite by surprise. But when I couldn't I had another way of surprising him, and I think it surprised him still more."

"Oh, what way was that, please, Mr. Grizzly Bear?" said Tommy Smith.

"Why, this," said the grizzly bear, and, as he spoke, he threw himself down on his back, and began to roll about, with all his four legs in the air. Then, all at once, he jumped up again, ran round in a circle, just as a kitten does after its own tail, turned head over heels two or three times, then rolled about, on his back, again, jumped up, and said: "There, that was my trick. I hope you think it was a clever one."

Tommy Smith thought it was a very clever *thing* for the grizzly bear to do all this (it had surprised and interested him very much indeed), but he didn't quite see how it was a clever trick. "Oh, Mr. Grizzly Bear," he cried, "I think it's very funny of you to do all that, but how did it catch the buffaloes?"

"Why, don't you remember my saying," said the grizzly bear, "that when the white men first came into my country I felt great curiosity about them, which was why I ran after them, because I wanted to look at them, only they were frightened and ran away. That was because I was not accustomed to them, so that seeing them was like seeing some strange new thing. Well, it was the same with the buffaloes. They had curiosity too—most animals have—and when they saw me going on like that, they wanted to find out what it was, because it was something they were not accustomed to. So they used to come up and look at me, and then I used to catch one of them."

"How many used to come up, to look at you, Mr. Grizzly Bear?" said Tommy Smith.

"Oh, I didn't set my trap for too many," said the grizzly bear. "That would have been dangerous for me. They used to go in immense herds, and if I had got into the middle of a herd I might never have got out again alive. But the herd would be dotted all about over the prairie, feeding, and I used to choose some place where the ground was broken, and there were not many near enough to see me. Perhaps a dozen or twenty would make a ring round me and begin to come nearer and nearer, getting more and more excited, till at last one of the bulls—because, of course, they were braver—would make a dash in at me, and then I had him, and the rest were so surprised, they ran away."

"How did you kill him, Mr. Grizzly Bear?" said Tommy Smith.

"Like this," said the grizzly bear. "I used to rear up on my hind-legs, catch him round the neck with my paws, in this way, and fix my great teeth in his muzzle. You see?"

Tommy Smith saw very well indeed, for the grizzly bear went through it all, just as if he had a buffalo in the cage with him. "Oh, yes, I see, Mr. Grizzly Bear," he said. "But didn't he kill you, sometimes, because he was a bull-buffalo, and bull-buffaloes are so strong, you know, Mr. Grizzly Bear."

"Oh, yes, I know," said the grizzly bear, "and the bull-buffalo that I caught used to make a very strong jump, to get away, only then I used to give a jerk with my head—like this—which was strong too, so strong that it threw him down, and then I lay all along him, so strongly that he couldn't get up again."

"Of course you were so heavy, Mr. Grizzly Bear," said Tommy Smith. "But had you still got your teeth in his muzzle?"

"Up till then I had," the grizzly bear answered, "but as soon as I had him down, like that, I fixed them in his throat instead, and tore it open."

"Oh, Mr. Grizzly Bear!" said Tommy Smith. "And did you pull his neck over to one side as well?"

"I dare say I may have done sometimes," said the grizzly bear, "but that would have been something extra."

"Because the lion does that with the buffalo, in Africa, you know, Mr. Grizzly Bear," said Tommy Smith.

"Well, we each have our plan," said the grizzly bear. "Mine was what I told you, but that wasn't my only one. Another was to throw one of my great forearms over his neck, and to seize his muzzle with my other paw—in this way (both the great paws of the grizzly bear came through the bars of his cage, as he showed Tommy Smith how he did it), and at the same time—look now!—I would draw up the hind-foot that was nearest to him, and rip him right open with these long, strong claws of mine."

"Oh, Mr. Grizzly Bear!—and, of course, that killed him," said Tommy Smith.

"Nothing more was required," said the grizzly bear. "Sometimes my claws would tear away some of his ribs, at the same time, but that was extra, too."

"But couldn't the buffalo-bull do anything, Mr. Grizzly Bear?" said Tommy Smith.

"Very little after that," said the grizzly bear.

"No, I don't mean then, of course, Mr. Grizzly Bear," said Tommy Smith. "But didn't he ever wound you or drive you away?"

"If he ever got away himself he was lucky," said the grizzly bear, "but it wasn't often that he did, because, you see, he was taken by surprise."

"But you didn't always play a trick like that, to catch him, Mr. Grizzly Bear, did you?" said Tommy Smith.

"Whether I did or not," said the grizzly bear, "I always took him by surprise, and although a full-grown bull-buffalo is a very large and powerful animal, yet he is no match for a large male grizzly bear."

"You must be strong, Mr. Grizzly Bear," said Tommy Smith.

"Fairly robust," said the grizzly bear, and then continued: "That was in the old days, as I told you, but as there are no more buffaloes for us now, we grizzlies have altered our diet, a good deal. Sometimes we take an ox or a cow—tame buffaloes those are, you know— and we play the very same trick upon them that we used to upon the wild ones. White men who look after cattle have sometimes seen us. Then sometimes, if we're lucky, we may get a moose or a wapiti, but, for the most part, now, we live upon roots, berries, grasses, prairie-turnips, marmots, ground-squirrels, and things of that sort. In fact, we have become vegetarians."

"Yes, that's all very fine, Mr. Grizzly Bear," said Tommy Smith, "but marmots and ground-squirrels are not vegetables, you know, so you're not vegetarians if you eat them."

"Well, well, I didn't mean strict ones," said the grizzly bear. "You see, they're quite small, and we have to dig for them, just as if they were roots, so it's natural to think of them in the same way. Are you sure they're not roots?"

"Yes, of course I am, Mr. Grizzly Bear," said Tommy

Smith. "They're animals, and you know they are. It doesn't matter how small an animal is, and as for their going to sleep in their holes, in the winter, so that you have to dig them up, don't you hibernate too, Mr. Grizzly Bear?" He had always heard that bears go to sleep in the winter, and he knew the right word for it, because the squirrel had told him.

"Oh, yes, I 'den up,'" said the grizzly bear. "That's what I call it."

"Yes, but you're not a vegetable, Mr. Grizzly Bear," said Tommy Smith.

"I might just as well be till I wake up again," said the grizzly bear.

"In the spring, Mr. Grizzly Bear?" said Tommy Smith.

"Yes, not till the spring," said the grizzly bear. "It's very exhausting to have to sleep so long, and I'm a very different bear when I wake up again."

"How do you mean, Mr. Grizzly Bear?" said Tommy Smith.

"Why, I'm very fat when I go to sleep, and very lean when I wake up," said the grizzly bear. "You see I've only my fat to eat whilst I'm asleep, and it isn't enough for me."

"You don't eat it, Mr. Grizzly Bear," said Tommy Smith. "You only live on it, you know."

"I call that the same thing," said the grizzly bear.

"That's how I live on roots and marmots and ground-squirrels. I eat them."

"Yes, but you don't eat your fat, Mr. Grizzly Bear," said Tommy Smith.

"Then, why is it gone when I wake up?" said the grizzly bear. "That proves it, I think."

"Oh, no, Mr. Grizzly Bear," said Tommy Smith. "You can't eat your *own* fat, of course, because it's on you, you see."

"It *was* on me," said the grizzly bear, "but when I wake up, it's gone. So I must have eaten it in my sleep. Why, how could I live on *any* fat without eating it? If you explain that, I'll alter my opinion."

Tommy Smith knew he was right, but he couldn't explain it, so the grizzly bear didn't alter his opinion. "What sort of den do you go to sleep in, Mr. Grizzly Bear?" he asked, instead of trying to get him to—for that would have been of no use.

"It's not always what you'd call a den, perhaps," said the grizzly bear. "Sometimes it's a hole that I have to scoop out myself, by a rock, and as much underneath it as I can. But what I like best is some natural cave in the side of a cliff. Of course, there must be a fir-tree or some juniper bushes or something else growing in front of its mouth, to hide it, or it would not be a good one. I should not make my bed in a cave that was not well concealed."

"Oh, you make a bed then, do you, Mr. Grizzly Bear?" said Tommy Smith.

"Why, you wouldn't have me sleep on the hard ground, would you?" said the grizzly bear, in almost a reproachful tone of voice. "I make a bed, of course."

"I didn't think you'd want one, with the thick coat you have, Mr. Grizzly Bear," said Tommy Smith.

"That's all very well for a blanket," said the grizzly bear, "but I want a mattress as well, and I make one of grass, moss, leaves, and the branches of trees that have fallen down. I scrape them altogether into my cave, even if I have to scrape them along, for a good way, before I get them there."

"It's very clever of you, Mr. Grizzly Bear," said Tommy Smith. "I suppose you each of you have your own den to sleep in, because you're so big."

"If it comes to that," said the grizzly bear, "there are caverns quite convenient for family use. But it's only the mother bear and her cubs who sleep in one, together. We male grizzlies like to have a den to ourselves."

"Oh, how many cubs does the mother grizzly bear have, Mr. Grizzly Bear?" asked Tommy Smith.

"Two is the usual number," said the grizzly bear, "but sometimes she has three or four."

"How big are they, at first, Mr. Grizzly Bear?" asked Tommy Smith.

"How big should you think they were?" said the grizzly bear.

Tommy Smith looked at the great animal he was

talking to, and then said: "Perhaps they're as big as a very large cat, or—or a terrier dog, Mr. Grizzly Bear."

"They're about nine inches long and weigh about half a pound," said the grizzly bear. "Of course they've no hair on them then, and they're quite blind."

"Oh, that *is* small," said Tommy Smith. "Are they—are they pretty, Mr. Grizzly Bear?"

"So their mother thinks," said the grizzly bear.

"And so they are," said a very sleepy voice from somewhere at the back of the cage. Tommy Smith was very much surprised, but the grizzly bear looked more surprised still, and said: "Well, that *is* wonderful. It shows what her feelings are, because *she's* denning up, inside there. As for myself, I don't find the winter here cold enough, but she keeps up old customs."

"Oh, but won't she come out now, and talk about the cubs?" said Tommy Smith. "Now that she's begun to," he added.

"It must have been in her sleep," said the grizzly bear. "It shows what her motherly heart is. But I don't think you'll see her or hear her again, because she's denning up."

And he was quite right. The female grizzly bear didn't say anything else after that, and Tommy Smith was so disappointed that he left off talking about the cubs. "Why should she go to sleep all the winter, Mr. Grizzly Bear," he couldn't help asking, in rather a discontented tone of voice, "if it isn't cold enough?"

"You see, there's so little to do here," said the grizzly

bear. "It would be better, I sometimes think, if we could both of us go to sleep altogether. But one has to wake up again, of course, and I should be afraid of dreaming of things I like doing, and missing them more when I woke up and found I couldn't do them. I'm sure I should dream of salmon-fishing, and there's none to be had here."

"Salmon-fishing, Mr. Grizzly Bear?" said Tommy Smith.

"Yes," said the grizzly bear. "They're the only fish worth eating, *I* think, and catching them is almost more fun than eating them."

"Oh, but however do you catch salmon, Mr. Grizzly Bear?" said Tommy Smith.

"Why, with my paw, to be sure," said the grizzly bear. "You see, in my country, ever so many salmon come up the rivers in spring and autumn. Autumn is the best season, because the water is clearer and shallower then—so shallow that sometimes their backs, where they are all pressed together, come right up out of it. I come down to the water, where it is shallow like that, and walk out upon the trunks of some fir-trees that have fallen into it, from the bank, and got jammed together—that is always happening where I live. When I have got to just the right place, I sit down with one of my paws hanging over in the water, and, as a salmon comes by, I make a scoop with it, and throw it right out of the water, so that it falls on the bank."

"Oh, how clever of you, Mr. Grizzly Bear!" said Tommy Smith. "Just fancy a bear catching salmon!"

"Yes, just fancy," said the grizzly bear, "and just fancy three or four of us together, out on the same trees, and all fishing at the same time, in different places, with first one fine large salmon, and then another, flying through the air in a high cloud of spray, with the sun shining on its scales, and making the water-drops sparkle. Such a silver and gold shower! There's no finer sight, *I* think."

"Oh, I wish I could see you doing it, Mr. Grizzly Bear," said Tommy Smith.

"You wouldn't want to kill us when you saw us doing such an interesting thing, would you?" said the grizzly bear. "I mean when you're grown up. Of course you wouldn't now."

"Oh, no, Mr. Grizzly Bear," said Tommy Smith. "I shan't ever want to kill animals when I grow up, but only to watch them and see the interesting things that they do."

"That's right," said the grizzly bear, "and, of course, you quite understand that when we grizzlies catch salmon, we do it to get our living, and because it's part of our natural way of getting food, and not just because we like catching them."

"Oh, yes, Mr. Grizzly Bear, I understand that," said Tommy Smith.

"We like catching them because we like eating our dinners," said the grizzly bear.

"Yes, Mr. Grizzly Bear, that's why, of course," said Tommy Smith.

"Of course it is," said the grizzly bear. "Well, good-bye

for a little." And he began to saunter towards his den, for although he wasn't going to hibernate, that was no reason why he should not have a little nap. Just before going inside, he half looked round, and said in a quite sleepy voice: "Of course, it's amusing for us grizzly bears to catch salmon, but that's a very different thing from catching them for amusement. The difference is——— Only I can't keep awake now, so I'll tell you another time."

Then he went into his den, and all at once Tommy Smith remembered that he had not seen the kangaroo yet, so he set off to find him as fast as he could.

CHAPTER V

THE KANGAROO

TOMMY SMITH had very often heard of the female kangaroo's having a pouch to carry her young in, and that was what he wanted most to see and talk about, and he kept thinking of it on his way to the kangaroo cages. And he was very lucky, because the first thing he saw, when he got to where they were, was a mother kangaroo jumping about on the grass-plot, at the back of them, and this mother kangaroo had a young kangaroo in her pouch, and its head was looking right out of it.

"Oh, Mrs. Kangaroo," he cried, "I am so glad you've got your baby with you."

"Baby!" said the mother kangaroo. "He's not a baby, now, any longer. Jump out, child, and show that you're not." And as she said this, the little kangaroo jumped right out of its mother's pouch, and began to jump about over the grass-plot, too.

"Oh, it does look pretty, Mrs. Kangaroo," said Tommy Smith. "But can it get into the pouch again easily?"

The Kangaroo

"Nothing simpler," said the mother kangaroo. "Here, child, you're wanted. Danger, Joey—danger!" And, at the word "danger," the little kangaroo gave a startled look, and came bounding up to its mother, and, with a last bound, disappeared just for a moment, because its head came out again almost directly.

"Oh, how pretty!" said Tommy Smith, for the second time. "But you called it Joey, Mrs. Kangaroo. Then is that its name?"

"It's what people call it in Australia, which is the country I live in," said the mother kangaroo, "so sometimes I call it so, myself."

"I think it's very clever of it to get in like that," said Tommy Smith.

"Sometimes it's very clever of me, too," said the mother kangaroo.

"Of you, Mrs. Kangaroo?" said Tommy Smith.

"Yes, because I help it—don't I, Joey?" said the mother kangaroo.

"You didn't help it, then," said Tommy Smith.

"It was not necessary," said the mother kangaroo. "But when there really is danger, and I'm running as fast as I can, to get away from it, then I have to help Joey as he gets up, or perhaps he would fall on to the ground, and be left behind, if I didn't stop and wait for him, and that would waste very precious time. Well there, then, you may go, child." This, of course, was to Joey, who jumped out, and began to play about on the grass once more.

"But how can the little one get to you, Mrs. Kangaroo, when you're running like that?" said Tommy Smith. "Because, of course, you run much faster that it does, so that it would never catch up to you."

"Not unless I were to let it," said the mother kangaroo, "but I go a little slower, at first, on purpose to. Then, sometimes, when it's playing about by itself, we run to each other, and, as we meet, up it jumps, just at the right time, so that I hardly have to slacken my speed for an instant. It makes its little bound, and I catch it and help to put it into my pouch, and it helps to put itself in, too, and we both do it at the same time, and off we go together again, with hardly a moment lost. I'll show you that, too, if you like."

"Oh, I should so like you to, please, Mrs. Kangaroo," said Tommy Smith.

"Danger, Joey—danger!" cried the mother kangaroo again, and she bounded towards her young one, who came bounding to her, and then it all happened just as she had said. The child kangaroo gave a jump into the mother kangaroo's pouch, and the mother kangaroo caught him between her forepaws and put him in just at the same time that he put himself in, but whether he put himself in more than she put him in, or she put him in more than he put himself in, Tommy Smith couldn't feel quite sure about. But as there was no real danger, the little kangaroo was soon out again.

"I suppose you're running away from some other animal when you have to run like that, Mrs. Kangaroo," said Tommy Smith. "What animal is it, please?"

"Well, it might be those horrid wild dogs, the dingos," said the mother kangaroo, "but much more often, now, it's horses with men on their backs, and dogs, larger and fiercer even than dingos, that run in front of them, longing to tear us to pieces."

"But can they run faster than you, Mrs. Kangaroo?" asked Tommy Smith.

"Oh, yes, they catch us," said the mother kangaroo. "Not always, of course—we manage to get away sometimes, but much more often we're caught and torn to pieces."

"I wish you could always get away, with your young one, Mrs. Kangaroo," said Tommy Smith.

"Oh, that's the worst part of it," said the mother kangaroo. "If only I could save little Joey! But, you see, if I can't save myself I can't save him, so what's the use of keeping him too long?"

"Then doesn't he stay in your pouch whilst you're running away, Mrs. Kangaroo?" said Tommy Smith.

"Oh, for a long time he does," said the mother kangaroo—"sometimes all the time, if I can get away with him, but when I can't, then I have to dispouch."

"Does that mean that you have to put him out, Mrs. Kangaroo?" said Tommy Smith. He thought it a funny word.

"Oh, yes, it does. I wish it didn't," said the poor mother kangaroo, looking very distressed.

"I think that's dreadful, Mrs. Kangaroo," said Tommy Smith.

"I do it as gently as I can," said the mother kangaroo.

"Then the poor little kangaroo is killed by the dogs?" said Tommy Smith.

"Poor little Joey!" said the mother kangaroo.

"I wonder how you *can* do it, Mrs. Kangaroo," said Tommy Smith.

"So do I, every time," said the mother kangaroo. "But, you see, when a poor mother kangaroo is chased by dogs, with a lot of men and women on horses, behind them, yelling and cracking their whips, she's very frightened, and she longs—oh, she does long so to get away. To be torn to pieces by dogs' teeth is such a dreadful death to die—she knows how dreadful it is because she has seen it happen to other kangaroos. How can she save herself and Joey too? Only by putting him into her pouch, and that will make it more difficult for her to save herself—for he's heavy now, poor little Joey is—and, of course, she can't run so fast whilst she's carrying him. But she wants to save Joey even more than she wants to save herself—at least she thinks so then, poor mother—so she does put him into her pouch, and away she bounds. But the dogs keep getting nearer and nearer, and as she hears them barking closer, and closer, behind her, she gets more and more frightened, and Joey get heavier and heavier, and she thinks: 'Oh, I must throw Joey out or I'll be caught.' And so she's going to, but then she thinks: 'Oh, I *can't* throw him out, because then he'll be caught.' And so she doesn't, but the dogs get nearer, and Joey—oh, Joey's so heavy now, and she's going to, again, but she can't, again; and then she looks round and sees the teeth, and, all at once, she's going faster, leaping more lightly, speeding away like the wind, for oh! she *has* thrown Joey out, and the white teeth that made her do it are in him, and stained with his blood. They're tearing Joey to pieces."

"Poor mother kangaroo!" said Tommy Smith. He wondered afterwards why he didn't say, "Poor Joey!"—but that was what he did say.

"You see, they make me do it," said the mother kangaroo.

"You mean the dogs do, Mrs. Kangaroo?" said Tommy Smith.

"Oh, it's not the dogs, really, or the horses either," said the mother kangaroo. "It's the cruel men and women who ride the horses and urge on the dogs. They make me do it, and when I have done it, do you know what they say?"

"No, Mrs. Kangaroo," said Tommy Smith.

"Why, they laugh and say that now I've 'dinged the Joey!'" said the mother kangaroo.

"'Dinged the Joey!'" cried Tommy Smith.

"They call my young one the Joey, you know," said the mother kangaroo.

"Yes, I understand that word," said Tommy Smith, "because it's just a name, and not new at all. But the other's such a funny word."

"It's one they've made themselves," said the mother kangaroo. "The people where I live like to make funny words for funny things. They think my having to throw away my poor little child, to save myself from the dogs, is a funny thing, and so they call it 'dinging the Joey.' And yet those very people who make me do it have often little children of their own, and some of them *must* be named Joey. Mustn't they?"

"Oh, yes, I suppose so, Mrs. Kangaroo," said Tommy Smith.

"That seems to make it more shocking," said the mother kangaroo. "Don't you think so?"

"I don't know," said Tommy Smith, "but I think it's horribly cruel of them, whether they've got children or not, and whatever their children's names are. But do you only have one little baby kangaroo, Mrs. Kangaroo?" he asked.

"Only one at a time," said the mother kangaroo.

"Oh, that is a pity, Mrs. Kangaroo," said Tommy Smith, "because they would look so pretty jumping and playing about together."

"Oh, you can see them doing that without their being brothers and sisters," said the mother kangaroo. "We kangaroos are fond of each other's society—well, it's the best, you know—and often, in the great heat of the day—and it's very hot in my country—if you come to an open glade amongst the trees and bushes that grow all about there, you may see quite a number of us gathered together. Some of us grown-ups will be lying asleep or dozing, in the sunshine, and others feeding quietly, in the shade, whilst our young ones—the Joeys—frisk about, play at fisticuffs with their pretty little front paws, jump up at one another, and sometimes, when they're very audacious, go right over each other's backs. Ah, what a pretty sight it is!"

"I should like to see it, Mrs. Kangaroo," said Tommy Smith.

"When they are a little older, but still young," the mother kangaroo continued, "you may see them all together in a flock, without any old one at all. They have left their parents, the pretties, and now they keep house for themselves. They are very lively then, too, though beginning to reflect a little, to learn that life is not all play, and that they are not Joeys any longer."

"But don't you go on calling your young one 'Joey,' Mrs. Kangaroo?" said Tommy Smith.

"I couldn't call him anything then," said the mother kangaroo, "because, you see, he would have left me, and even if I were to see him again, I should hardly know him amongst fifty others, perhaps."

"Fifty others!" cried Tommy Smith.

"Quite that, sometimes, or even more," said the mother kangaroo. "But, however, even if I did know him, I should not call him Joey then."

"Oh, wouldn't you, Mrs. Kangaroo?" said Tommy Smith.

"At least, I should make an effort not to," said the mother kangaroo. "Only, you see, he would be in his flock, then, and I would be in mine, so we should not be likely to meet any more."

"Then do kangaroos live in flocks?" said Tommy Smith.

"To be sure we do," said the mother kangaroo, "and to see a great flock of us bounding over the country is a splendid sight. You don't see it properly unless we're startled. When we're browsing about quietly we get scattered, and no one would think how many of us there were. But as soon as anything startles us, off we go, all bounding away together, all following the one that goes first, which is usually an old male."

"Is he the leader?" asked Tommy Smith.

"As long as he can go first, he is," said the mother

kangaroo. "When he's tired of going first, then he drops out, and the one that was just behind him goes first instead. When we go in these great flocks, no one can stop us or make us turn back. We may swerve to this side or that, for a little, to get out of anybody's way, but still we will keep going the same way that we were going. We never think of turning round."

"But if people hurt you, don't you turn round, Mrs. Kangaroo?" said Tommy Smith.

"Oh, no," said the mother kangaroo. "It's they who have to turn round and follow us. If any rude people come and stand in our path when we're jumping along in a flock, like that, the flock divides and goes one on each side of them. There are two flocks then, but they can't be kept separate for long, because, as soon as they have left the rude people behind them, they join together and make one again, never fear."

"But why do you always want to go just one way, Mrs. Kangaroo?" said Tommy Smith.

"It's the way we were going, you know," said the mother kangaroo, with rather a puzzled look, Tommy Smith thought.

"Yes, Mrs. Kangaroo," said Tommy Smith, "but is it the way to some place that you're going to?"

"Oh, yes, it's certain to be," said the mother kangaroo. "It must go to some place that we're going to, of course."

"No, but I mean does it go to some place that you want to get to, Mrs. Kangaroo," said Tommy Smith. "I don't mean any place."

"Oh, if it comes to that, one place will do as well as another," said the kangaroo, "because, you see, the country's all alike."

"Yes, but then, why won't you go another way than the way you were going, if people come and frighten you, Mrs. Kangaroo?" said Tommy Smith.

"Oh, we shouldn't think of it," said the kangaroo. "You see it's the way we were going, and so we keep on in it, of course. No one can make us go another way. Can they, Old Man?"

"Certainly not, Doey," said a much larger kangaroo that had just come jumping up. "That would not do at all."

"No, it wouldn't, would it, Old Man?" said the female kangaroo.

"It would not, Doey," said the male kangaroo (for, of course, it was the male), in the same grave tone of voice. (He seemed very serious-minded.) "But where's Joey, Doey?"

"Not very far off, Old Man," the female kangaroo answered. "Joey!" And Joey came jumping up from somewhere, and sat between the two, for a little, before he jumped into his mother's pouch again. So there was the family circle.

"Oh, Mrs. Kangaroo," said Tommy Smith, "why do you call the male kangaroo 'Old Man'? And why does he call you 'Doey'?"

"Why, those are the names for us in Australia," said the female kangaroo. "Every full grown male kangaroo

is an 'Old Man' there, and every female kangaroo is a
'Doey.' So he's my 'Old Man' because he's my husband,
and I'm his 'Doey' because I'm his wife. That's right,
Old Man, isn't it?"

"Certainly, Doey," said the male kangaroo. "But one
subject at a time. We hadn't quite finished about our
not turning back."

Tommy Smith thought that he and the mother
kangaroo had finished. But what the male kangaroo
meant was that he had not begun, and it was quite clear
that he wanted to.

"Our idea is," the male kangaroo continued, "when
we have once made up our minds to do a thing, to
go through with it, and not let anyone turn us from
our course. So if we have made up our minds to go
north, we go north, if south, south, and so on. Now
the natives of Australia—the 'black fellows' as they call
themselves—know what a firm character we kangaroos
have, and they take advantage of it in a very mean way.
Instead of just running after us, and throwing their
spears at us, from behind, which would give us a fair
chance of getting away, because we go so much quicker
than they do, a lot of them get in front of us, and stand
about where they think we are likely to come. Then
when we do come, first one will throw his spear at one
of us, and then another, some way behind him, will
throw his, and in this way they may kill several of us,
before we have passed them all. But we don't turn back
and go another way, because of that. We're not turned
from our course. Are we, Doey?"

"I should think not, Old Man," said the female kangaroo. "They can't make us do that, however many of us they may spear."

"Not even if they were to spear all of us," said the male kangaroo.

"But if they were to spear all of you, it would have been much better if you had turned back, Mr. Kangaroo," said Tommy Smith.

"Better!" said the male kangaroo. "Why, we should have lost our firmness of character."

"But you'd all have been alive, anyhow, Mr. Kangaroo," said Tommy Smith.

"Yes, but going the wrong way," said the male kangaroo, with quite a horrified look.

Tommy Smith saw that it was no use trying to argue with animals that had an idea like that in their heads. He remembered, now, that, in some of the natural history books, it said that kangaroos were not very clever, and besides, it was always better to ask animals questions than to argue with them—they were so obstinate. So he said: "Is it always with spears that the black men in Australia hunt you, Mr. Kangaroo?"

"With spears and boomerangs," said the male kangaroo. "Those are their two weapons. But perhaps you don't know what a boomerang is."

"Yes, I think I do, Mr. Kangaroo," said Tommy Smith. (He had heard his father talk about them.) "Isn't it a piece of wood that's shaped like a bow, only more bent, and you throw it, and then it comes back to where you threw it from?"

"Yes, and it's most unfair," said the female kangaroo. "If it hits us, it may break one of our legs, perhaps, or hurt us very much in some other way, or even kill us. But if it misses us, there it is, almost directly, in the man's hand who threw it, for him to throw at us again. I don't see any justice in that."

"Don't you, Doey?" said the male kangaroo.

"No," said the female kangaroo, "and I don't believe there is any."

"You shouldn't say that, Doey," said the male kangaroo.

"Can't help it, Old Man," said the female kangaroo.

"Without spears, boomerangs, dogs, horses, black men, and white men," said the male kangaroo, very gravely, "what would be the use of kangaroos having firmness of character? Firmness of character, if there were not enough things to be firm about, would be wasted."

"But there oughtn't to be more than enough," said the female kangaroo.

"It has to be properly exercised," said the male kangaroo, "and that accounts for the spear-thrower, too."

"I don't think that's so bad as the boomerang," said the female kangaroo, "but it isn't fair either."

"It accounts for everything of that kind," said the male kangaroo. "Do you see it now, Doey?"

"Not quite," said the female kangaroo, "but I'm beginning to feel it." And the male kangaroo gave a satisfied look at Tommy Smith, and said: "She's in the right road."

"But what is a spear-thrower, please, Mrs. Kangaroo?" asked Tommy Smith.

"Why, it's something those 'black fellows' make, to throw spears with," said the male kangaroo. "Instead of just throwing them with the hand as you would, but not at us, I trust (of course Tommy Smith said, 'Oh, no, Mr. Kangaroo'), they hold a stick, and throw it with that."

"Oh, but how, Mr. Kangaroo?" said Tommy Smith.

"You see, this stick has a sort of point at one end, which turns backwards," said the male kangaroo, "and at the end of the shaft of the spear, there is a little round hole into which that point fits. The native, when he throws his spear, fixes the point of the spear-thrower into the hole of the spear, and holds the other end of it in his hand. Then, when he brings his arm forward, the stick throws the spear, and the spear goes a great deal farther than if he had thrown it with his hand, without the stick. I don't know why it should—I never could quite understand it. But it does—it's a well-known fact."

"I think it's very clever of him, Mr. Kangaroo," said Tommy Smith—though he didn't understand it either.

"It's a false arm—that's what I call it," said the female kangaroo, "and I don't like men who use false arms. Why they should be better than their real arms I'm sure I don't know, but they are, and I think it's a very unfair advantage. Spears are dangerous enough, without spear-throwers to make them more dangerous. I've often thought how unfair it is and wondered why it should be; and boomerangs that go back of themselves, to be thrown at us again, are more unfair still. Then there are the white men, with their guns and their horses and dogs, and the sheep that they've brought with them, to eat up the grass that was meant for us to eat—all very unfair, to say nothing of dingos and poisonous snakes, and all sorts of other trials. Oh dear, I get tired of it all, sometimes, and if it wasn't for Joey here—yes, that's right, child (for Joey had jumped into his mother's pouch again—he was always in and out)—I should begin to think the world was a very funny place, and wonder why it's all what it is."

"If it were not what it is," said her husband, very gravely indeed, "there would be less firmness of character in us kangaroos, and we mightn't jump as well, either. That is the answer, Doey."

"Yes, I feel it is now," said the female kangaroo, "but I think it's Joey as well. There, run away and play, child (and Joey jumped out again), for I should like to go to sleep till feeding-time."

"So should I, Doey," said the male kangaroo—and they both of them jumped off to their cage, which had a sleeping-place at the back of it.

Tommy Smith would have liked them to stay and talk with him, a little longer, but there was no turning either of them from their course.

CHAPTER VI

THE OSTRICH

ANOTHER of the animals that Tommy Smith wanted to have a conversation with was the ostrich, and whilst he was wondering how he should find him, all at once he saw him walking up and down beside the bars of the quite small enclosure, which was all he had to come out into when he was tired of being inside his "house," and wanted a walk or a run. He knew it was the male bird, directly, because of the handsome black feathers of his body, and the beautiful white ones in his wings. He might have known it too, after a little, by the way in which the blood showed through the veins of his neck, whenever he was at all excited, giving it a reddish hue under the white downy feathering.

"I suppose you know who I am?" said the ostrich, as soon as Tommy Smith got right up to him.

"Oh, yes, of course, Mr. Ostrich," said Tommy Smith, "there's no other bird so——"

"Oh, there's no mistaking me," said the ostrich. "And I dare say you know something about me too."

"Oh, yes, Mrs. Ostrich," said Tommy Smith, "I know

that you lay your eggs in the sand, and that you don't sit on them, yourself, to hatch them, but leave them to be hatched by the sun. And I know that when you see anyone you're frightened of, and don't want him to see you, you hide your head under the sand so that you can't see him, and then you think he can't see you either. And I know that when you want to run very fast, you spread out your wings, like sails, for the wind to catch them and blow you along, and I know——"

"Stop!" said the ostrich (he had been getting more and more red in the neck as Tommy Smith went on, just as a man who is getting angry might get red in the face. "You don't really know all that, you only think you know it."

"Oh, no, Mr. Ostrich," said Tommy Smith, "I'm quite sure I do, because it's in all the natural history books."

"Then you'd better not read any of them," said the ostrich, "because it's all nonsense, and I think I ought to know, as I'm 'The Ostrich' myself."

It certainly seemed as if the ostrich should know something about it, so Tommy Smith hardly knew what to say or think, for here was what his father would have called "a conflict of authorities."

"Isn't any of it true, Mr. Ostrich?" he said at last.

The ostrich paused, a little, to consider, and then said: "You see, it's all so mixed up. Sometimes, when I begin to run, I do spread my wings and hold them high up on each side of my neck, like this, and then off I go with high, springy, bounding steps, in this style—There's

The Ostrich

really not room here, but I'll do what I can." And so he did, and very handsome he looked, too, going round his paddock in that way. By holding his wings out, he showed the long, soft white feathers in them, that we all know so well, to the very best advantage. Tommy Smith was very much interested. It was really one of the finest sights he had ever seen.

"Only, you see," continued the ostrich when it was over, "all that has nothing to do with using my wings as sails. I don't do that at all. If I did I should always have to run the way the wind was blowing."

"But don't you, sometimes, Mr. Ostrich?" asked Tommy Smith.

"It's only by chance when I do," replied the ostrich, "and, as a matter of fact, I prefer to run against the wind. I don't know why, but somehow I do. I think it must be good for my throat."

"For your throat, Mr. Ostrich?" said Tommy Smith. No wonder he was a little surprised.

"It feels so nice and fresh about it," said the ostrich— "so cooling after the great heat of the sun. But, however, that's only an idea of mine. The great thing I have to consider, when I run, is getting where I want to get to, and as long as I do that, I don't much mind how the wind's blowing. It blows just as it likes, you know, and very often if it were to blow me along, it would blow me the wrong way. So now, please remember that when I spread out my wings in that way, it has nothing to do with the wind."

"But why do you spread them out, then, Mr. Ostrich?" said Tommy Smith.

"I couldn't always say, exactly," said the ostrich, "but generally it's when something startles me. You see, I'm rather nervous and high-strung, and though I can't fly, any little surprise throws me into a flutter, and off I start like that. But that doesn't last long. Soon I settle down into a long, raking stride——"

"Please, what does 'raking' mean, Mr. Ostrich?" said Tommy Smith.

"Upon my word," said the ostrich, "I hardly know

how to describe it. In fact I'm not sure that I know what it means, but it's *the* word, and there isn't any other one that will do instead. Long, raking strides. 'Steady' might give you an idea, but that doesn't sound so well. No, 'raking,' if you please—that's the word. They're—well, I'll show you." And off the ostrich went again. Oh, how he did run now! It was quite a different thing. Before, when he spread his wings out, he had held his head about as high as usual, Tommy Smith thought, but now he lowered it so that his neck made a great loop, which kept moving as if it had been a snake, but Tommy Smith noticed that his head was quite steady and did not shake at all. As for his wings, they were not spread now, but lay along his sides, only just enough out from them not to get in the way of the upper part of his legs, for, of course, that would have hindered him. He went ever so much faster now, almost as fast, Tommy Smith thought, as if he had really been flying round and round his little paddock, which was a great deal too small for such a performance, so that when he stopped, all at once, just in front of him, and said he felt giddy, Tommy Smith was not in the least bit surprised.

"Well, how did you like it?" the ostrich asked. "I'm sorry it was such a slow affair."

"Slow!" cried Tommy Smith. "But I know you don't mean that really, Mr. Ostrich, because you went like lightning."

"Ah, you should see me in the desert," said the ostrich. "I don't mind running in a wide circle—it's what I generally do, in fact—but there's no going fast in such a narrow one. Well, did you notice my wings as I walked round this time?"

Tommy Smith knew that the ostrich spoke like that just for fun, so he only said: "Oh, yes, I did, Mr. Ostrich. You didn't hold them out at all."

"If I had," said the ostrich, "their resistance to the air would have been so great that I could only have just crawled. Even in the desert I couldn't go really fast—not what *I* call fast—if I were to spread them as people say I do. Then my head—you saw how steady I kept it?"

"Oh, yes, Mr. Ostrich," said Tommy Smith. "It didn't move at all."

"If I didn't hold it quite firm, I couldn't see properly," said the ostrich. "But however fast I go—and I do go fast in the desert—I can look about me quite calmly and see all that's happening. Well, now you know how I really run, and what I do and don't do with my wings. As for that other silly story about my hiding my head in the sand, I'll explain that too. You see, in some parts of the desert where I live, I am hunted for my feathers by the Arabs, who live there too, and although one man on horseback would never run me down, yet when there are a good many they sometimes manage to do it, because, you see, I run in a circle and not in a straight line. That's my way."

"Isn't it a funny way, Mr. Ostrich?" said Tommy Smith.

"Not at all," said the ostrich. "It's just what you would do, if it were not for roads. If you were lost anywhere,

where there were no roads, and nothing to guide you, when you tried to get home you would walk right round in a circle. Well, these Arabs, by knowing how I run, are able to judge where I shall have got to, after a certain time, and so a party of horsemen go off there and wait for my coming, whilst the others are chasing me, and as they go straight to the place, whilst I am making a great circle, they get there long before I do, and have time to wait and rest their horses. When I get near to them, they come galloping out, and meanwhile another party has gone on to wait for me somewhere else, where they know I shall get round to, and they keep doing that, till at last I am quite exhausted and have to lie down, with my neck stretched straight out in front of me, because I can't hold it up any more. So, of course, in that way I do put my head on the sand, but as for putting it under the sand and trying to hide myself like that, as they say I do, I should never think of doing anything so absurd."

"Oh, I see, Mr. Ostrich," said Tommy Smith. "Then you don't try to hide at all?"

"What would be the use of my trying," said the ostrich—"on those open plains and with the horsemen close after me? I should be very glad to hide in a rational manner, if I only knew how. But as for that nonsensical story, it makes me quite angry to think of it. Hide my head in the sand indeed! To think you should believe such things about me!"

"I don't now, Mr. Ostrich," said Tommy Smith, "and I'll tell every one I see that it's not true."

"Pray, do," said the ostrich. "Enough mischief has

been caused already by the spread of such a report, and there is no saying what may happen if it is allowed to go further. Well, now I'm ready for some questions."

"I suppose the Arabs would never catch you, Mr. Ostrich," said Tommy Smith, after thinking a little, "if they only just rode after you, and didn't go to where they knew you were coming?"

"Never," said the ostrich. "If it was a fair chase, with the same horses all the time, I should just run right away from them, because I go so much faster. But with fresh horses that have gone on before, waiting for me first at one place and then at another, I haven't a fair chance. Still, even with that, it isn't often that they get me. I generally succeed in making my escape."

"Are you really the fastest animal that there is, Mr. Ostrich?" asked Tommy Smith.

"In my native wilds, I am," said the ostrich.

"But can you run faster than an antelope, Mr. Ostrich?" said Tommy Smith.

"There are all sorts of antelopes," said the ostrich, "and I can run faster than the fastest of them all."

"Which one is that, please, Mr. Ostrich?" asked Tommy Smith.

"Suppose we say the gemsbuck," said the ostrich. "He's the fastest in South Africa, and I consider South Africa my headquarters. Farther north there are others— the oryx and the oribi—that run just as fast, but they're all very like one another, and I can run faster than any of them."

"But how fast can they run, Mr. Ostrich?" said Tommy Smith.

"About twice as fast as anything fast you can think of—as long as you don't think of me," said the ostrich. (Of course he was exaggerating.)

"Then can you run faster than a zebra, Mr. Ostrich?" said Tommy Smith.

"A zebra? Of course I can," said the ostrich impatiently. "Why, he doesn't run so fast as a gemsbuck. Didn't you ask me if I was the fastest animal that there is? And didn't I tell you that I was? If I'm the fastest of all, I must be faster than any of them, so it's no use keeping on asking me whether I'm faster than this one or that one. Why, when I'm running really fast, the length of my stride is from eleven to fourteen feet, and I can make three strides in a second. No animal can beat me, but here are two *things* where I live that sometimes manage to go faster than I can."

"What two things are they, Mr. Ostrich?" asked Tommy Smith.

"The wind and the poisoned arrows of the Bushman," answered the ostrich.

"Oh, Mr. Ostrich," cried Tommy Smith, "does the Bushman shoot you, too?" (he was not at all interested in the wind). "He shoots the lion, you know, because the lion told——"

"No wonder," said the ostrich, "I don't think much of *him* as a runner."

"He comes up to him whilst he's asleep, Mr. Ostrich,"

said Tommy Smith. "I don't think he could catch him by running. Of course I know he can't run like you, only just for a little, after he's got close to any animal, he can run almost as——"

"You needn't tell me about the lion," said the ostrich. "I know all about him, much better than any little boy can do. As for his being shot by the Bushman, he deserves it, for he's a cruel, murderous animal, who comes up to me and kills me when I'm asleep and can't kick him. If that were all the Bushman did I should have nothing but praise for him, but he shoots me, too, though I'm harmless, and he does it in the meanest way that could possibly be imagined."

"Oh, yes, Mr. Ostrich," said Tommy Smith, who remembered something he had read now. "Doesn't he dress himself up with your feathers, and——"

"It's more than that," said the ostrich. "If it were only my feathers I might have some chance. Any ordinary disguise I could see through, but when he makes himself part of me, and shoots me from inside myself, no wonder I'm deceived."

"From inside yourself, Mr. Ostrich?" said Tommy Smith. "Do you mean that——?"

"He skins me," said the ostrich in a tone of strong feeling, "and then he puts my whole skin right over him, with a stick through my neck, so that he can hold it up, with my head in the proper place. That makes me the outside part of him, and him the inside part of me. All except my legs, because he's cut those off, but he paints his own legs so as to look like mine. At least their colour does; of course *as* legs they're contemptible. If it were not for the rest of me I should notice them directly, but all the rest is so exactly the same—because, you see, it is the same—that it's just as if it were me—I mean, all me, right through, you know. And then he's so cunning that he imitates everything we ostriches do, and comes up to a group of us just as if he belonged to it and had strayed away for a little. At one time, he puts down his head to the ground, and then lifts it up, just a little, and puts it down again, as if he were feeding, and at another, brings it right round amongst his feathers—only, they're really mine—as if he were preening them with his bill—my own bill. He keeps making me do what I would do myself if he hadn't killed me. Of course we don't suspect him—how could we? So he gets gradually nearer to us—not as though he wanted to very much, that might make us uneasy, but just by chance, that's what it seems like—oh, the most perfect acting—till, at last, he's right amongst us. Then, all at once, he goes into an odd attitude, and a little white thing comes out of the feathers of his breast, and then there's a twang and a whiz, and one of us has a poisoned arrow sticking in him. Oh, there was never such an act of treachery."

"I suppose you all run away then, Mr. Ostrich," said Tommy Smith. (He knew that the little white thing which the ostrich saw was the bone point of the arrow.)

"Certainly not," said the ostrich. "You see we don't know what it is yet, and it would not be very dignified to run away until we knew what we were running away from. We see that something has happened, and that something is the matter with one of us, but what it is we don't know. So we all hope that bird will get better, and go on feeding."

"And then, does the Bushman shoot another of you, Mr. Ostrich?" said Tommy Smith.

"Yes, indeed, the wicked little creature," the ostrich answered. "You see, it's impossible to suspect him, because, directly afterwards, there he is, walking and feeding about again, just like an ostrich amongst other ostriches. Sometimes he'll even pretend to be startled himself, as if *he* wondered what had happened too, and then gradually quiet down again, just like us. Oh, he is cunning."

"What does the ostrich that has been shot do, Mr. Ostrich?" said Tommy Smith.

"He falls down very soon," said the ostrich, "and, one after another, there may be three or even four of us struggling on the ground. However, no one can hope to take in ostriches for ever, and though we've still no idea that a Bushman with his arrows is amongst us, we feel sure now that there is something not quite what it ought to be about this new ostrich. Then all at once, just as one of us, perhaps, is going to run at him and kick him, there's no ostrich there, where he was, but, instead, a horrid little yellow man, shooting arrow after arrow at us, as fast as he can. Then at last, when we've discovered him, we make off, and are soon speeding away, far beyond the reach of such a wretched little short-legged creature."

"I suppose he takes the ostrich-skin off him, Mr. Ostrich," said Tommy Smith.

"Yes, he throws it down on the ground," said the ostrich, "and as quick as he can, too, because he knows if he didn't he'd be kicked. To escape that, he has to confess himself beaten."

"But he's killed some of you, you know, Mr. Ostrich," said Tommy Smith—for this was quite a new idea to him.

"That may be," said the ostrich. "But we've found him out and exposed him, which ought to make him thoroughly ashamed of himself."

"If you'd found him out at first, Mr. Ostrich——" Tommy Smith was beginning.

"That would have been better of course," said the ostrich. "Still our turn has come, and when one does win, one mustn't mind winning at last. That's the way in which I see it."

Tommy Smith didn't see it at all in that way, because *he* thought the Bushman had won. But after all, it was only *his* opinion, and it was better for the poor ostrich to have quite a contrary one, because it made him happier. So instead of trying to show him that he was wrong, which was one of the most difficult things to do, with animals, he just went on with the conversation. "Please, Mr. Ostrich," he said, "do ostriches kick each other when they have a fight? Because you said you were just going to kick the Bushman, before he threw off your skin, and you thought he was an ostrich then."

"Quite right," said the ostrich. "Yes, we do kick each other, and very hard too."

"Like a horse, Mr. Ostrich?" said Tommy Smith.

"No," said the ostrich, with dignity, "not like a horse. A horse kicks backwards. We should be very sorry to do *that*. In fact, I don't think an ostrich *could* do it."

"Couldn't he, Mr. Ostrich?" said Tommy Smith.

"I hope not," said the ostrich. "You see, we're not made like that. Kick backwards! Why, to do that, one would have to turn one's back to the enemy, and I should think that a very cowardly manner of fighting."

"But one turns one's back when one runs away," said Tommy Smith, "and you do run away, you know, Mr. Ostrich."

"That's another thing," said the ostrich. "One's not obliged to fight, of course, but if one does, one should do so in a proper manner. Horses may do what they like, but when we ostriches fight, we advance upon each other, breast to breast, like true warriors, and when we kick, we kick forwards."

"Could you show me how you do, please, Mr. Ostrich?" said Tommy Smith.

"Something like this," said the ostrich. And, on the instant, one of his feet shot up into the air, a good deal higher than Tommy Smith's head, and came down with a thud, on the ground, like a hammer. Then the other went up and came down in the same way, and then the other again, and so on, quite a shower of kicks, each one so hard that, if it had been against a door, Tommy

Smith felt sure that the ostrich's foot would have gone right through it. The only wonder was that he didn't hurt his feet against the ground, only it was not really there that he made the kick, but in front of him, at about the height of his own breast, so that if it had really been a fight they would have fallen on the breast of the bird fighting him. Tommy Smith was very much interested. He had never had any idea that ostriches fought in this way. In fact, he had not thought about their fighting at all.

"There," said the ostrich, stopping, a little out of breath—of course he was not in good practice—"I've done as well as I can for you, in such a one-sided affair. I'm sorry not to have been able to make it a little truer to life. However, I've only my wife here, and that would not quite do."

Tommy Smith didn't quite understand what the ostrich meant at first, but when he did, he was very glad to think it would not quite do. He would have felt very uncomfortable if it had. "I didn't know your wife was here, Mr. Ostrich," he said, after he had thanked him for the exhibition. "Do you think she'll come out?"

"I think she is coming out now," said the ostrich. And sure enough, as he said so, the much less handsome grey body of the hen ostrich appeared in the doorway of her house, and, the next moment, she was stalking towards them.

"Tommy Smith, my love," said her husband, as she came up, "that boy, you know, who's so very fond of talking to animals. Now," he continued (but this was to

Tommy Smith), "if you still think we leave our eggs to be hatched by the sun, and don't sit on them, you can hear what she has to say about it."

"Not sit on them!" cried the hen ostrich—she was excited in a moment, so that she forgot even to say, "How do you *do?*" "Of course we sit on them. I should like to hear anybody tell me not to sit on them. Not sit on my own eggs indeed! I do sit on them, and if he didn't, too" ("he," of course, meant the male ostrich), "oh, how I should despise him. We both do. How dare anybody——However, you're only a little boy."

Tommy Smith was very glad that the hen ostrich ended in this way, because he thought she was going to put her head through the bars, and peck him. He would have moved away, only that might have made her more angry.

"It's the natural history books, you know, dear," said her husband. "The child's not to blame."

"They ought to be burned, that they ought," said the hen ostrich, "spreading such mischievous falsehoods. Oh, what must people think of me? What must they be thinking of me, at this very moment? Oh, what a cruel slander."

"I don't think you don't sit on them, now, Mrs. Ostrich," said Tommy Smith, feeling very uncomfortable indeed.

"Thank you," said the hen ostrich. "It's rather late in the day—but thank you."

"If we *were* to leave our eggs to be hatched in the

sun," said the male ostrich, very gravely, "they would never be hatched at all. In our country the sand gets so hot, in the sun, that, if you were to lay your hand on it for more than a few seconds, the skin would be blistered. Without us to cover them, our tender little chicks would get so hot in their cradle that they would soon be dead. They might be roasted in that way, but they would never be hatched."

"Oh, what a dreadful picture!" said the hen ostrich, and Tommy Smith agreed with her.

"The sun's all very well in his way," the male ostrich continued, "but he has to be well looked after. At certain times of the day, when he's not quite so hot, we allow him to help us a little, but as for putting the entire care of our little ones into his hands, that would not do at all."

"Not to be thought of," said the hen ostrich. "Besides, he'd never expect it."

"Not for a moment," said her husband. "He has his regular duties and we have ours."

Tommy Smith thought this a funny way of talking, as if the sun were really alive. But he knew that if the ostriches really thought so, it would be no use to explain to them that he wasn't, and besides, he was anxious to hear something about the young ostriches, and how they were hatched and brought up. So he only said: "Then you both sit on your eggs, Mr. and Mrs. Ostrich?" so as to give them the opportunity.

"Oh, yes," said the male ostrich, "we take it in turns."

"Yes, he's very good," said the hen ostrich, "and

always ready to help me in my arduous task. I begin, of course. I look upon that as my right. At the proper time in the morning—about your breakfast-time, I should think—I take my place upon the nest and sit there, all alone with my treasures, till about your tea-time."

"Oh, that is a long time, Mrs. Ostrich," said Tommy Smith.

"Then he relieves me," said the hen ostrich, "and I get a scanty meal."

"I hope you get enough, my dear," said the male ostrich. "You know you're so clever at finding things."

"I'm not complaining," said the hen ostrich. "What mother would not sacrifice herself for her children?"

"And how long do you sit on your eggs, Mr. Ostrich?" asked Tommy Smith.

"His! They're mine," said the hen ostrich.

"Quite right, my love," said the male ostrich. "They're yours, of course, but you let me sit on them all through the night, till you come again in the morning."

"That's how it's divided," said the hen ostrich. "I wake and watch on them, all day, and he goes to sleep on them, all night. But what mother would think of complaining?"

"But it's light a long time before I go off and after I go on," said the male ostrich. "You should remember that, dear."

"Oh, my dear, if I were complaining I would," said

the hen ostrich, "but you know I'm not. What mother would? We help each other in making my nest, too," she continued, turning to Tommy Smith. "He does the scooping out the sand part and the kicking it away with his feet—the spade-work as one may call it—whilst I stand over him and encourage him by fluttering and clicking my wings—which, of course, is an art."

"Clicking them, Mrs. Ostrich?" said Tommy Smith. "However do you do that?"

"Like this," said the hen ostrich, and she really did click them in a very curious way. Besides this, she bent down her head and took up a little of the soil, in her beak, and then lifted her head up again, and let it fall. "I do that for him too," she remarked, after she had repeated the act several times.

"Perhaps you would like to see how I make her nest," said the male ostrich. And without waiting for Tommy Smith to say, "Oh, yes, please, Mr. Ostrich" (which, of course, he did), he went right down on his breast and began to scrape the ground away, with his feet, behind him, in the most curious manner.

"That's the way we divide it," said the hen ostrich. "He works in the rough, whilst I add beauty and finish, which includes music."

Tommy Smith didn't think this description was quite fair to the male ostrich, but he didn't seem to mind it. In fact, he looked as if he would have smiled if he could. It was evident that the two quite understood one another.

"What are the little ostriches like when they first come out of the egg?" was Tommy Smith's next question.

"Oh, the prettiest, sweetest little things," said the hen ostrich. "Only don't ask me to describe them, because I couldn't do them anything like justice."

So Tommy Smith didn't. "They begin to run about directly, I suppose, Mrs. Ostrich?" he said instead.

"Whoever can have told you that?" said the hen ostrich. "But I suppose it's the books."

"Not a doubt of it," said the male ostrich.

"Run about directly!" said the hen ostrich. "No, indeed they don't. At first they're so helpless they can't even hold up their heads, though I'm sure they've every reason to. Their necks and the back of their poor little heads are all swollen and out of shape. So are their legs— puffed up like a jelly, they are, and half-transparent. How could they walk, with them in that state? All they can do, at that tender age, is just to lie in the nest and look beautiful."

"Yes, I see, Mrs. Ostrich," said Tommy Smith. He did see how fond their mother must be of them, to think that.

"Twenty-four hours have to go by, before they can stand, even," continued the mother ostrich, "for walking, another day is required, but when they do begin, they're worth seeing."

"They are," said the male ostrich.

"Oh dear," said the hen ostrich, "they can hardly

136

make two steps without falling, and go tumbling over each other in the most fascinating way. You see, before they can even walk properly, their poor, pretty, little, swollen legs must go down. After that, the stronger ones begin to wander away from the nest, a little, with one of us to look after them, and soon they all leave it, with both of us."

"Oh, then you both of you look after them, Mrs. Ostrich?" said Tommy Smith.

"To be sure we do," the hen ostrich answered, "and we both advise anybody not to interfere with them."

"Would you both kick them?" Tommy Smith asked.

"That would be more his duty," the hen ostrich answered, with a glance at her husband, who made a sudden, loud hissing, which quite startled Tommy Smith, and, at the same time, gave a violent kick or two. "My part, requiring tact and management, would be more to get them away. But, if necessary, I should be prepared to do anything. So people had better be careful."

"I wish you had some young ostriches here, Mrs. Ostrich," said Tommy Smith.

"What would be the use?" said the hen ostrich. "There's nowhere to go with them here, and nothing to show them. We haven't our beautiful, free, wide-stretching desert, to take them out into."

"Oh, the desert!—the desert!" burst out the male ostrich. "The lovely, parched plains that stretch and stretch for ever: the blue haze, like water, in the distance, that dances and dances, and that you rush and rush on towards, but never get to: the hot air that sings, as you bound through it: the hot sand you just touch and leap up from. Oh, the desert!—the desert!"

"And the nest—the nest in it," said the hen ostrich, "where I sit, all day, in the beautiful, burning-hot sunshine, thinking of you and the eggs, and what's going to happen to them. And then, as the rays slant and slant, and I feel that my feeding-time's coming, but don't want to go till you come, there's just a black speck in the distance, ever so far away, and I know it's you, even when I can hardly see it, and it gets larger and larger so quickly, and soon I see that it is, and then you come running up. Oh, the desert!—the desert!"

"Then you don't mind it's being so hot there, and the sand, and there not being real water, and—and what other people mind, Mr. and Mrs. Ostrich?" said Tommy Smith.

"Mind!" said the male ostrich. "Why, we're made for it. It's our beautiful home. Just look at that foot." And he held it up for Tommy Smith to see closely.

"It's a very funny foot, Mr. Ostrich," said Tommy Smith, after looking at it carefully. "It's only got two toes, and one of them's ever so much larger than the other, and has a big nail. The other has hardly got any."

"That foot," said the male ostrich, proudly, "stands alone, amongst birds. No other bird's has less than three toes, but that grand toe of mine has got so used to running that it can almost run by itself. The other only just helps it, a little. The toe of the desert, I call that toe.

It's the one we kick with, too, mostly, so it wants that large, strong nail." And he put down his foot again, after Tommy Smith had had quite a long look at it, and felt it with his hands.

"What do you eat in the desert, Mr. Ostrich?" asked Tommy Smith.

"Oh, many kinds of plants and leaves," said the male ostrich, "and we have to walk a good long way for them, too, for, in the desert, things don't grow very thickly. Then there are lizards, small tortoises, snakes, young birds, and a number of other delicacies. We ostriches like a mixed diet."

"Do you swallow the tortoises with their shells, Mr. Ostrich?" said Tommy Smith.

"To be sure," said the male ostrich. "Why, how could we get them out of it? You've heard of our digestion, I suppose."

"Oh, yes, I have, Mr. Ostrich," said Tommy Smith.

"It's a grand one," said the ostrich.

Then he looked a little away—as though he were trying to see the desert, Tommy Smith thought—and said: "Don't think me rude, but the last few sentences have made me feel as if I could do a little pecking, now. Come, my love, I feel chilly. Perhaps we have both of us stood a little too long, at the bars."

And, with an easy nod to Tommy Smith, the two great birds moved away and began to pry about, on the ground, towards the center of their enclosure. As it was not the desert, or at any rate not the right kind of one, Tommy Smith wondered what they would be able to find there. There did not seem to be anything, but perhaps they had really gone away because they had had enough conversation, for the present. So he called out: "Good-bye, Mr. and Mrs. Ostrich," and went away himself.

CHAPTER VII

THE WILD BOAR

THE next conversation that Tommy Smith had was with the wild boar. He didn't consider him such a very interesting animal, but he was lying so close against the bars of his cage, that he could hardly have gone by and not have said anything, without its seeming rude. Besides, when he saw Tommy Smith, he lifted up his head, a little, and gave a grunt that sounded quite friendly.

"Oh, is that you, Mr. Wild Boar?" said Tommy Smith. He couldn't think of anything else to say, just at the beginning.

"Yes, it is," said the wild boar, "and it has been for quite a long time—in fact, ever since I was myself."

"I only meant that—that I thought it was, Mr. Wild Boar," said Tommy Smith.

"You were quite right," said the wild boar.

"Of course I knew it was you, really, Mr. Wild Boar," Tommy Smith explained, "because——"

"Oh," said the wild boar, "I thought you asked the question."

The Wild Boar

Tommy Smith saw that the wild boar was not clever at conversation, and that the only way was to help him a little, or else they would never get on. So he tried to think of the right thing to say, but, whilst he was trying, the wild boar went on with:—

"Perhaps now you would like to ask me some more questions." That made it a little easier to help him, and he said at once: "Oh, yes, Mr. Wild Boar. Do tell me something about your habits, please."

"All my habits?" said the wild boar.

"Oh, no, not all—unless you like, Mr. Wild Boar," said Tommy Smith, "but your most interesting habits."

"Sugar-cane," said the wild boar.

"Sugar-cane?" said Tommy Smith.

"That's it," said the wild boar.

"But that's not a habit, Mr. Wild Boar," said Tommy Smith.

"Eating it is," said the wild boar.

"Oh, is that what you mean, Mr. Wild Boar?" said Tommy Smith.

"That's it," said the wild boar. "It's quite the best of my habits, except, perhaps, one other, and that's ripping."

"Ripping, Mr. Wild Boar?" said Tommy Smith. "Oh, do you mean with your tusks?"

"Of course I do," said the wild boar. "What else should I rip with? Sugar-cane and ripping—there are those two."

"But you must have some more habits, you know, Mr. Wild Boar," said Tommy Smith.

"Sorry I'm obliged to," said the wild boar, "but you said the most interesting. Well, shall I tell you about them?"

"Yes, but with other things too, Mr. Wild Boar, please," said Tommy Smith. "How you live, I mean, and what you do every day."

"I go to sleep every day," said the wild boar.

"But that can't be all you do, surely, Mr. Wild Boar?" said Tommy Smith.

"Oh, I wake up from time to time," said the wild boar, "and doze before going to sleep again."

"But I didn't know you were a nocturnal animal, Mr. Wild Boar," said Tommy Smith.

"I didn't either," said the wild boar, "but those are my habits in the day-time. You can see them if they interest you." And he stretched himself out on his side, as if he meant to go to sleep directly.

"Oh, but what do you do in the night-time then, please, Mr. Wild Boar?" said Tommy Smith very quickly, before he could shut his eyes. He thought the wild boar was the very worst animal for a conversation of any that he had spoken to.

"Oh, the night, is it, now?" said the wild boar. "Well, that's better. About dusk I rouse myself, and sally forth from where I've been lying hidden all day, in a thick patch of bushes with long grass all round it, in the bed of a nullah or by the edge of a swamp, or——"

"What is a nullah, Mr. Wild Boar, please?" asked Tommy Smith.

"That's what we call it in India," said the wild boar. "It's a sort of gorge or deep valley, with steep hills on each side of it, and we wild boars will always get into one, if there are any about."

"Oh, then, do you live in India, Mr. Wild Boar?" said Tommy Smith.

"The finest and largest of us do," said the wild boar. "We are at our best there, but we inhabit other countries as well, both in Asia and Europe. Well, about dusk, as I was saying, we leave our nullah and go to places where sugar-cane is to be found. Have you ever eaten sugar-cane?"

"Oh, no, Mr. Wild Boar. It doesn't grow in England, you know," said Tommy Smith.

"To think I should have been put into such a country," said the wild boar. "There are whole plantations of it where I come from, and to get into one, just when it's ripe, and know you have all the night before you, is to feel that life has a meaning."

"Do you eat it all night, Mr. Wild Boar?" asked Tommy Smith.

"All night," said the wild boar, "and when we get back to our nullah again, in the quite early morning, what a lot we have eaten, to be sure. Oh, those nights! Ten feet high or more the canes are, sometimes, but we just give a jerk up with our heads, to one side and another, and our tusks go through them with such a beautiful, clean-cutting sound, and they come swishing down all about us, and over our backs and heads, and then it's just squish, squash, munch, munch, munch, munch, munch, all the night through. Just try to think of it—squish, squash, squish, squash, the juice spurts out on each side of our snouts—some of it's wasted, well, that can't be helped, we get it back, lots of time and no hurry—squish, squash, munch, munch, munch— squish, squash, munch—"

"Oh, I do think you're greedy, Mr. Wild Boar," said Tommy Smith.

"Greedy! I should think so," said the wild boar. "Oh, the delight of it! Greedy, and all night to be greedy in, and greedy on sugar-cane!"

"But aren't there other things you like, besides sugar-cane, Mr. Wild Boar?" said Tommy Smith.

"When we can't get sugar-cane, there are," said the wild boar, "acorns and ground-nuts, rice, corn, millet, barley. Oh, and walnuts—walnuts! To have them lying all scattered about under those great handsome trees that they grow on, and to go trotting off, with the sounder, at the right time of year for a walnut feast. Oh, walnuts—I should think so! But sugar-cane!! Squish, squash, squish——"

"Oh, don't make that noise any more, please, Mr. Wild Boar," said Tommy Smith. "I do think you're the greediest animal that——"

"Yes, that's all very well," said the wild boar, "but what good does it do me here? It's so wasted."

"But you are fed here, you know, Mr. Wild Boar," said Tommy Smith.

"Just once every day, in the day-time," said the wild boar, "and never on sugar-cane. It isn't like India."

"You can't always be feeding, in India, even when it's on sugar-cane, Mr. Wild Boar," said Tommy Smith. "You must have some other habits, you know."

"Shall we come to the ripping?" said the wild boar.

"No, not yet, please, Mr. Wild Boar," said Tommy Smith—he didn't want it all to be about eating and fighting. "What did you mean when you said about trotting off with the sounder? That's such a funny word, you know, Mr. Wild Boar."

"Oh, that means all of us together," said the wild boar. "You see, ordinary animals go in herds or flocks or troops or droves, and so on, but we wild boars are not ordinary animals, so we go in sounders."

"That is funny, Mr. Wild Boar," said Tommy Smith.

"I should think it funny if we did not," said the wild boar. "You can't expect us to be mixed up with deer or sheep or buffaloes, as we should be if we went in a herd or flock."

"Not if you kept in a herd by yourselves, Mr. Wild Boar," said Tommy Smith.

"Oh, but it wouldn't be a herd then," said the wild boar. "It would be a sounder."

"Yes, you call it that, Mr. Wild Boar," said Tommy Smith.

"Always call things by their right names," said the wild boar, "but if you prefer herds to sounders, the buffalo lives over there."

"Oh, no, I don't want to go to him yet, Mr. Wild Boar," said Tommy Smith. "How many of you are there in a sounder, then?"

"Oh, that all depends," said the wild boar. "There are large sounders and small ones. Sometimes forty or more of us will go trotting over the country together— or it may just be a family party."

"Oh, I should like to see the little pigs trotting about with you, Mr. Wild Boar," said Tommy Smith.

"Not so much with me," said the wild boar. "I'd be

there, and, in case of danger, would be ready to defend them, of course. But further than that I can't go."

"Can't you, Mr. Wild Boar?" said Tommy Smith.

"No," said the wild boar, "for personal attention they must look to their mother."

"You mean she looks after them, Mr. Wild Boar?" said Tommy Smith.

"That's her duty as well as her pleasure," said the wild boar. "A kindly look and a kindly grunt I always have for them, but she must make their hut."

"Their hut?" cried Tommy Smith—he was very much surprised.

"Yes," said the wild boar. "It would be no use my trying to help. I should be afraid of eating it."

"Eating it!" cried Tommy Smith, still more surprised than before. "Oh, whatever do you mean, Mr. Wild Boar?"

"Why, you see," said the wild boar—he had rather a shamefaced expression, Tommy Smith thought—"the hut is often made of sugar-cane."

"Oh, is it, Mr. Wild Boar?" said Tommy Smith. Of course he understood that part of it now.

"Yes, that's why," said the wild boar. "Of course, I shouldn't want to, and I'm sure I'd do my best to struggle against the temptation, only it might be too strong—I don't know."

Tommy Smith thought he did know, especially as

the wild boar began to move his jaws a little, as if they would soon be making the sound of "squish, squash, munch, munch," again. But he was more interested in the other part of what the wild boar had told him, so he said: "But how does the mother wild boar make a hut for her young ones? Do tell me that, Mr. Wild Boar."

"Oh, in the cleverest way you can think," said the wild boar. "She goes cutting and cutting and cutting, till she has made quite a litter of sugar-cane, and then, with that delicate snout of hers—my own's rude and clumsy compared to it—she lifts it up, all round them and over them, as they lie on it, and over herself too, till she and her family are inside a hut."

"But how does she make it stand up?" said Tommy Smith.

"That you must ask her," said the wild boar. "I can make a rude shanty, for myself, of grass and fallen branches, but where the children are concerned I leave it entirely to her."

"Just as it ought to be," said the female wild boar, who, at this moment, came trotting out of the little inner compartment at the back of the cage, where she had been all the while. Perhaps she had been asleep till now, but if she had, it was funny she should have woken up at just this part of the conversation, and Tommy Smith felt sure she had been listening. "Just as it ought to be," she repeated. "If you were to make a hut for them, and live with them in it, I dare say, when you came out and left them there, you'd forget to shut the door after you."

"Yes, or I might eat it," said the wild boar—but this was in a low voice.

"The door!" cried Tommy Smith. "Oh, but has your hut a door to it, Mrs. Wild Boar?"

"Has it, indeed!" said the female wild boar. "I should not consider it a hut if it had not."

"But how do you open it and shut it, Mrs. Wild Boar?" asked Tommy Smith.

"In this way," said the female wild boar. "When I've lifted the sugar-canes up over them, and got them to stand properly——"

"Oh, but how do you do that, Mrs. Wild Boar?" said Tommy Smith.

"I couldn't tell you exactly," said the female wild boar. "It's done with a turn of the snout."

"Of that wonderful snout of a sow," said the wild boar. "We poor boars——"

"Then when I've made it," continued the female wild boar, "I make a window to look out of, by putting my head through the sugar-canes."

"Oh, is that what you call a window, Mrs. Wild Boar?" said Tommy Smith.

"It is, as long as I want it to be one," said the female wild boar. "When I have to go out and leave my family indoors, then, of course, I want a door, so I make the window into an open door by going through it, and when I'm outside I throw up some more sugar-cane, which makes it into a shut door, and then I feel I can go off in peace."

"Oh, I see, Mrs. Wild Boar," said Tommy Smith, "but that isn't quite like having a door, and opening and shutting it every time you go in and out, and then the window——"

"It's having an open door when you want it open, and a shut one when you want it shut," said the female wild boar, "so it comes to the same thing. As to the window, it's one when you don't want a door, and it's a door when you don't want a window, and when you don't want either, it's neither. *I* call that a flexible arrangement."

"You won't improve upon it easily," said the wild boar.

"I think it's very clever of you, Mrs. Wild Boar," said Tommy Smith. Really, he thought the *very* clever part of it was her closing up the hole, which she called a door, after she had come outside. But it was not necessary to explain this.

"It's wonderful what she does for the squeakers," said the wild boar.

"Don't speak of your children in that way, dear, please," said the female wild boar. "I don't like it at all, and you know I don't."

"But, my dear, it's the common name for them," said the wild boar.

"That's why I dislike it so," said the female wild boar. "Horribly common, I call it."

151

"Oh, but do they call the little wild boars squea——"
Tommy Smith was beginning.

"Pray don't repeat it," said the female wild boar (so,
of course, Tommy Smith didn't). "They do, but they
oughtn't to. Oh, how can they call such little angels,
with orange and white stripes all down them, by such
a name? How can they? How can they?"

"Oh, Mrs. Wild Boar," cried Tommy Smith (he was
so excited that he did not even think about trying to
answer her question, though she had asked it three
times), "are the little wild boars really striped like that?—
with orange and white, Mrs. Wild Boar?"

"Yes, that they are," said the female wild boar, "and
the stripes run all along their sides and backs."

"Right over from one side to the other, Mrs. Wild
Boar?" said Tommy Smith.

"Not that way, not that way; that would never do,"
said the female wild boar, hurriedly. "They run the way
their backs run, from their dear little heads to their dear
little tails—bless them!"

"You can't tell it's not the other way," said the wild
boar.

"Don't be so horrid—I can," said the female wild
boar. "As their mother, I feel that it is as I say."

"I should like to see them, Mrs. Wild Boar," said
Tommy Smith.

"Would you promise not to call them that, if you
did," said the female wild boar.

"Oh, yes, Mrs. Wild Boar," said Tommy Smith.

"Then you should see them if there were any here to see," said the female wild boar.

Tommy Smith felt very grateful, but even more disappointed.

"What do *you* call them, Mrs. Wild Boar?" he asked.

"Angels," said the female wild boar.

"Come, come, dear," said the wild boar, a little impatiently.

"You won't say that's not what they look like," said his wife, "striped in that way."

"Oh, but the tiger's striped something like that, you know, Mrs. Wild Boar," said Tommy Smith, "and you don't call——"

"Don't talk to me of that devil," said the female wild boar. "He'd eat them if he could, and me too."

"Oh, but can't he, Mrs. Wild Boar?" said Tommy Smith. "Because, you know, the tiger's so——"

"You needn't tell me anything about him," said the female wild boar. "I know what he is, and what his crimes are, for we roam the same forests. He can kill a full-grown bull-buffalo and sometimes even a younger-grown bull-bison, which is the strongest animal anywhere in our country, after the elephant and rhinoceros; and two tigers together have been known to attack and kill a cow-elephant. As for me and my children, he'd always be killing us, I think, only luckily" (she said this with great pride) "I have a husband, and they have a father."

"Now it's my turn again," said the wild boar. "Ripping now. That's my other great habit, you know."

"Oh, but can you fight a tiger, Mr. Wild Boar?" said Tommy Smith.

"Can he, indeed! He often does," said the female wild boar. "He's the bravest animal that there is in the world."

"Tut, tut," said the wild boar, "and all about a tiger. Why, I'd as soon fight a tiger as look at him."

"Then you're very foolish, because it's not nearly so safe," said the female wild boar.

"But wouldn't he kill you, Mr. Wild Boar?" said Tommy Smith.

"Of course, he does kill me sometimes," said the wild boar, "but more often I kill him."

"But he's so big, Mr. Wild Boar," said Tommy Smith. "And then he's got his claws and his teeth."

"These are my teeth," said the wild boar, and he made two quick digs in the air with his tusks, which seemed to make them flash. "As for claws, I can do without those. *I* only rip in one way."

"He is so brave," said the female wild boar.

"Does the tiger often attack you, Mr. Wild Boar?" asked Tommy Smith.

"Often," said the wild boar, "but not many tigers

attack me twice. You see, the first time they've had no experience. But when they've once had it, either they don't want it again, or they can't have it again."

"Do you mean because you've killed them, Mr. Wild Boar?" said Tommy Smith.

"If I don't kill a tiger, he usually kills me," said the wild boar, "and often we kill each other. But whether he kills me or not, if he gets away it's the last fight he'll ever want to have with a wild boar."

"I suppose you wound him so badly, Mr. Wild Boar," said Tommy Smith.

"I *rip* him," said the wild boar. "The best of it is," he continued, "that every tiger begins by not having experience, so that we wild boars are always having to give it them. In that way we get a good deal of ripping, at one time or another, though the pauses are often much too long."

"Don't speak like that, dear," said the female wild boar. "As the father of a family, you should not seek danger."

"Well, I don't," said the wild boar, "but it may seek me as much as it likes."

"That means he often runs into it," said the female wild boar. "Well, well."

"But do you really like fighting tigers, Mr. Wild Boar?" said Tommy Smith.

"Oh, very good ripping, very good ripping indeed," said the wild boar carelessly.

"Just hark at him," said the female wild boar.

"Do tell me about a fight, Mr. Wild Boar," said Tommy Smith.

"Let me see," said the wild boar. "You remember that time, my dear, when my wounds were so bad that I could hardly get back to you and the squeak——"

"Not if you say that, I don't," said the female wild boar.

"Anything you like, my dear—angels," said the wild boar.

"I should think I do remember it," said the female wild boar. "Bad wounds they were, indeed, and took a long time to heal."

"It was a good fight, and I've never forgotten it," said the wild boar. "I was digging for roots, I remember—with my snout, you know" (this was to Tommy Smith); "I turn up the ground with it, as if it were a plough. You should see my long furrows. But, however, I was digging for roots, as I say, in an open space just by the jungle—that's the word in my country for forest—and I remember I'd just turned out a beauty, when, all at once, I got a whiff of tiger, which made me throw up my head and stand still."

"A whiff of tiger? Of course you mean his scent, Mr. Wild Boar," said Tommy Smith.

"Of course I do," said the wild boar. "Such a strong whiff, and then, the next moment, there came a roar from the jungle, which almost seemed like a challenge."

"Oh, really—well, *that* wasn't your fault," said the female wild boar. "Well, go on, dear."

"I shall always believe it was meant for one," said the wild boar. "A challenge! My bristles were up in a moment, and I answered it in this way." The wild boar gave a loud and very curious kind of grunt that sounded something like "hoo, hoo," and quite surprised Tommy Smith. To make it, he lowered his head, and then flung it up and stood in a proud sort of way, Tommy Smith thought—just as if he were waiting for a tiger to appear. It was rather funny—of course it might have been only by chance—but the "Lion House" was not far off, and, just at that moment, there came a roar from it which did not sound quite like a lion's, but was much too loud for any other animal except a tiger. The wild boar seemed to have no doubt about it, for he made his loud "hoo, hoo," and flung up his head, again.

"Oh, Mr. Wild Boar, how splendid!" cried Tommy Smith. "I do wish the tiger was coming."

That was just what the wild boar was wishing too, only in a much more real way, and he really seemed to think that the tiger would come, for he "hoo, hoo'd" again, and, this time, made a dash forward, as if to meet him, so that he came right against the railings, and even struck them with his tusks.

"Good gracious, he'll hurt himself," said the female wild boar—and then to her husband: "Now, don't get excited, dear, please. Never mind his roaring" (for the tiger, if it was he, had given another roar), "you know he's not here, and can't get here."

The wild boar looked just a little shamefaced (Tommy Smith thought) and muttered something about its being "only for fun"—but, of course, that wasn't true. And then he looked as if he had forgotten there was anything more for him to talk about.

"Do go on, please, Mr. Wild Boar," said Tommy Smith.

"But not too much," said the female wild boar. "Not like that, again. You'll only break your tusks, you know."

"Was that how you attacked him, Mr. Wild Boar?" said Tommy Smith.

"No," said the wild boar. "It was only how I pretended to. I did that before he had quite come up to where I was."

"I suppose it was to show you were ready for him, Mr. Wild Boar," said Tommy Smith. "But what did you do after he had come up?"

"This is what I did," said the wild boar, and he began to turn slowly round and round, just in the one place where he had been standing—at least, he did not get far away from it. All the while he kept turning round like this, he seemed to be looking at something which was moving round him, and Tommy Smith felt sure that, if the fight had really been here, that something would have been the tiger. Of course he was very interested. "Oh, Mr. Wild Boar——" he was beginning.

"Shs!" said the female wild boar. "He'll tell you directly!"

"You see," said the wild boar, stopping and coming

158

up to the railings again—for he had chosen the middle of his cage to turn round in—"You see, the tiger keeps creeping and crawling round me, so I have to keep turning like that, so as always to have my head, with these little things in it, pointing towards him, to catch him on, when he springs. 'Ivories right!'—that's the word. Of course, if I were only just to walk round, in the same way that he does, my side would be turned to him, and he would spring in and claw me, all at once!"

"But can't you do that too, only with your tusks, Mr. Wild Boar?" said Tommy Smith, "because his side must be turned to you, you know, whilst he's walking round you."

"Ah, but then he's so quick," said the wild boar. "If I were to run in and try to rip him, he'd spring into the air, and come down on my back, very likely. And as for *his* head, he's like a snake, and can turn it anywhere, however he's standing."

"But why does he keep going round you, Mr. Wild Boar?" said Tommy Smith.

"Well, that's his idea," said the wild boar. "When you have a conversation with him, you can ask him why it's his idea, and, if he thinks it's a good one, then you can ask him how it was I won this fight I'm telling you about. He won't like that."

"How did you win it, Mr. Wild Boar?" asked Tommy Smith—for he knew that he would like that.

"I'll tell you," said the wild boar, "but no more questions till it's over, please. Well, all at once he was at me, but I was ready as he sprang, and though he gave me a stroke with his paw, which clawed my face badly and made me reel, I was steady again, in a moment, and got in three rips in his neck and chest. Dig—dig—dig—good deep rips they were—very good rips—and the blood came streaming out, as he turned and was off, with me charging after him."

"Oh, Mr. Wild Boar, you're beating him," said Tommy Smith.

"All in good time," said the wild boar. "I was close upon him—I'm a much swifter animal than you'd think perhaps, and I made such a rush—when, all at once, he slunk aside—he's so lithe and supple, you know—and I just missed my rip."

"Oh, Mr. Wild Boar, what a pity," said Tommy Smith.

"He took advantage of that, of course," continued the wild boar. "As I shot by him he flung himself round towards me, again, made his spring, and was right on my back, tearing and biting at me."

"The monster! How I hate him!" said the female wild boar.

"Oh, but what did you do then, Mr. Wild Boar?" said Tommy Smith.

"It was what he did, for a little," said the wild boar. "I could do nothing, for he lay all along me, with one of his paws on my face, all his five claws fixed in it, and trying to wrench round my neck, so as to break it."

"Oh, yes, the lion does that, Mr. Wild Boar," cried Tommy Smith.

"Only it was too strong," said the wild boar.

"So massive," murmured the female wild boar.

"Oh, I'm so glad he couldn't, Mr. Wild Boar," said Tommy Smith.

"I was, too," said the wild boar, "but how he did maul me, to be sure!" I felt faint through loss of blood, and began to think it was all over with me, when I stumbled and fell forward—and that saved me."

"I know how," said the female wild boar. Tommy Smith didn't know how and was going to ask, when the wild boar went on with: "Yes, it saved me, for he went right over my head, and lay sprawling in front of me, on the ground. That was my chance. My tusks were into him before he could get up again—it was dig, dig, rip, rip, rip, rip, rip—lengthways and sideways, across and across—and he never did get up again."

"Oh, had you killed him, Mr. Wild Boar?" said Tommy Smith.

"Never had such ripping in all my life," said the wild boar. "How I enjoyed it! It was sweeter than sugar-cane."

And without a word more—not even just to say good-bye—the wild boar turned his back and disappeared into his shed.

"He's gone to lie down and think about it," said the female wild boar. "He's like that—it always excites him."

"Oh, but won't he come out again, Mrs. Wild Boar?" said Tommy Smith.

"Good-bye, he wants soothing," said the female wild

161

boar. "But come again, another day, and he'll tell you some more of his battles." And with half a nod (if so much) to Tommy Smith, she went off, to look after her husband. Of course it was right that she should.

CHAPTER VIII

THE ORANG-OUTANG

AFTER his conversation with the wild boar, Tommy Smith thought that he would like to go to the Monkey House. But, on his way there, he remembered that the most interesting kind of monkeys are the apes, because they are larger and even more like men, and one of the keepers had told him that the apes were not kept with the other monkeys now, but had a house of their own. So he went to the Ape House first, and as the door that he went in by was nearest to the orang-outang, it was the orang-outang that he had the first conversation with.

"How like a man you are, Mr. Orang-outang," was either the first thing, or one of the first things that Tommy Smith said.

"I know what you mean," said the orang-outang, "only you haven't said it properly."

"Haven't I, Mr. Orang-outang?" said Tommy Smith.

"Not quite," said the orang-outang. "You might as well say how like myself I am (which would only be silly), because I *am* a man."

"Oh, but monkeys are not men, you know, Mr. Orang-outang," said Tommy Smith. He knew that animals were conceited, but he hadn't thought that any animal could be quite so conceited as that.

"Of course I know they're not," said the orang-outang, "and I should not think of calling you a monkey, only because you're like one."

"Oh, wouldn't you, indeed, Mr. Orang-outang?" said Tommy Smith.

"Certainly not," said the orang-outang, "so you oughtn't to talk about my being *like* a man either. It's the same for both of us, and I should not speak in that way of you. We may say we're like each other, of course, that's sensible."

"Sensible indeed!" said Tommy Smith angrily. He couldn't help feeling angry.

"Because it's true, but not too true," said the orang-outang. "That makes it sensible to say. When things are too true they sound silly. So don't say I'm like a man again, when I am one."

Tommy Smith didn't think that what the orang-outang thought was either true or sensible, but evidently he had a strong opinion, and he knew that when animals had strong opinions they didn't alter them because they were silly. However, he wasn't going to agree with him, so he only said: "What makes you think you're a man, Mr. Orang-outang?"

"It isn't thinking, it's knowing," said the orang-outang, "and that makes it worse. You see, it's my name,

The Orang-Outang

because orang-outang means man of the trees, or tree-man. Now that name was given me by the men who live in the country where I live, who, of course, must know much more about me than men who live anywhere else. If I wasn't a man they wouldn't say I was, but they see I am, so they call me so. There's no way of getting over that, is there?"

Tommy Smith felt sure that there was, but he was not quite so sure whether he had better say so or not, and whilst he was still making up his mind, the orang-outang went on speaking.

"That ought to convince anyone," he said, "or, at any rate, anyone who is not an orang-outang himself. But you see, I am an orang-outang, which makes me prejudiced, so if that were all, perhaps I might still think I was not a man—at any rate I should try to. But I'm sorry to say it is not all. Look at that. What do you call it? Do you call it a paw?"

"No, I don't, Mr. Orang-outang," said Tommy Smith. "I call it a hand."

"Yes, it is one," said the orang-outang—"there's no denying it. And what are these things I'm moving about? You needn't mind saying, because I know."

"Why, they're fingers, of course, Mr. Orang-outang," said Tommy Smith.

"Of course they are," said the orang-outang. "There's no way out of it. And *would* you call these nails or claws?"

"Nails they are, I'm sure, Mr. Orang-outang," said Tommy Smith. "They're not like real claws at all."

"Not at all," said the orang-outang, in quite a melancholy tone of voice. "And then look at these. Aren't they human?"

"Monkeys have ears like that, you know, Mr. Orang-outang," said Tommy Smith. He didn't say "other" monkeys, because he knew it would offend him.

"They're more pointed," said the orang-outang quickly. "But you needn't talk about monkeys, because *they* have tails."

"Yes, of course they have, Mr. Orang-outang," said Tommy Smith.

"Exactly," said the orang-outang. "You and I have not."

"I should think not, Mr. Orang-outang," said Tommy Smith indignantly. He must have meant it about himself, for, directly afterwards, he said: "But then, haven't you got one, Mr. Orang-outang?"

"The orang-outang shook his head sadly, and he even turned it away a little, as if he were ashamed of himself. "Not even a short one," he said. "I told you we were just like each other."

"I don't see that, Mr. Orang-outang," said Tommy Smith. "But I never knew you hadn't got a——"

"Please say nothing more about it," said the orang-outang. "It's a sore subject."

"Oh, very well, Mr. Orang-outang," said Tommy Smith, "but I think you might——"

"If you don't promise, I shall have to sit like this till you go," said the orang-outang; so, of course, Tommy Smith did promise. "Thank you. So dreadfully human," said the orang-outang. "Then, as for my face—well, I'll only ask you one question. Is this a high forehead or not?"

"Yes, it is a very high one, Mr. Orang-outang," said Tommy Smith, for it really was.

"Like a dome," said the orang-outang, "which is human, too—sadly human. Taken together, no wonder they call me a man."

"But why are you unhappy about it, Mr. Orang-outang?" said Tommy Smith. It seemed to him very funny that the orang-outang should first say that he was a man, and then seem not to want to be one.

"How can I help it," said the orang-outang, "when it seems to make me so wicked?"

"You needn't be wicked unless you like, Mr. Orang-outang," said Tommy Smith, "and men needn't either." Then he got quite angry with him, again—it was really so ridiculous—and said: "If you don't like being a man, I wonder you say that you're one."

"One should tell the truth even although it's against one," said the orang-outang. "Besides, there's no concealing it. With hands and arms—you must call these arms now, mustn't you?"

"Yes, they are arms, of course," said Tommy Smith, "but that doesn't——"

"They'd be legs if I were not a man," said the orang-outang, "and my real legs would be only hind-legs. No, with arms and legs like these, and with a face like this— these ears and this beard and whiskers and moustache (he pulled the hair out from the different parts of his face, and it did look very like all three), what use would it be to deny it?"

"Yes, but that isn't all your face, you know, Mr. Orang-outang," said Tommy Smith, "and there are parts of it not nearly so like a man's. Your nose is quite flat, you know."

"The proboscis-monkey may be more like a white man in that way," said the orang-outang. "But some men have very flat noses."

"Not so flat as yours, Mr. Orang-outang," said Tommy Smith.

"Oh, I've said that to myself, often," said the orang-outang, "but, you see, it's the same *kind* of flat nose, after all. No, I can't deceive myself. We're the same in all sorts of things, and when it comes to being clever—well, you know how clever some men are, and as for us orang-outangs, well, look here."

The orang-outang was sitting in a great heap of straw, and as he said, "Look here," he took up one of the straws in his hand, holding it by the stalk, just like a man, and pushed it out through the wires of his cage, till the end of it, where the ears grow, reached to the hot-water pipes. Just on the top of the highest pipe there was a sort of little tank with water in it, and the orang-outang was so skilful that he managed to dip the head of the corn-stalk into this water, and then he pulled it back and put it into his mouth and sucked. He did this several times, but he would not have been able to, perhaps, if he had not chosen a straw that was bent near the end—or perhaps he had bent it himself—so that when he pushed it far enough forward, over the edge of the tank, the head of it hung right down into the water. That, of course, made it all the more clever and skilful of him. "There," he said, after he had sucked it for the last time, "you've seen me do it, and now you can tell me what you think of it."

"Of course it's very clever of you, Mr. Orang-outang," said Tommy Smith.

"Yes, it wants a high forehead," said the orang-outang.

"And it's just what a man would do," Tommy Smith went on.

"Some men," said the orang-outang. "Still it shows I must be one."

Tommy Smith didn't think it showed quite so much as all that, but he knew it was no use arguing about it, so he only said: "I wonder you drink that water, Mr. Orang-outang. It must be quite warm, because there's steam coming out of it."

"You wouldn't wonder if you lived in the country where I live," said the orang-outang. "The sun is so hot there that water often gets warm, especially when there's only a little of it, and it's very high up."

"Very high up, Mr. Orang-outang?" said Tommy Smith.

"Yes," said the orang-outang, "because, of course, the nearer to the tops of the trees it is, the fewer leaves there are for the sun to get through."

It was no wonder that Tommy Smith didn't know what the orang-outang meant by this. It really didn't sound at all sensible. "One doesn't climb up trees, to get water, you know, Mr. Orang-outang," he said.

"I walk all about in them to get it," said the orang-outang, "or, at any rate, I go everywhere, and wherever I go I find it, either in one tree or another. You see, to begin with, there's the dew that hangs on the leaves, as I thought even a ground-man would know. That's very pleasant to sip, but what I like much better, when I'm really thirsty, is the little pools that the rain makes when it drops on to the branches, and runs down them to where they join on to the trunk. When the branches

170

are at all large there's sure to be a hollow place there, that the water stays in, and the great forests that I live in are full of trees so large and tall that their biggest branches are like tall trees themselves. That's where we find our beautiful large bowls of water—in the trees. You've heard of the boles of trees, I suppose."

"I think I've heard of the bole of a tree, Mr. Orang-outang," said Tommy Smith, "but——"

"There isn't only one," said the orang-outang. "Well, that's what it means, bowls of water in the trees for us orang-outangs to drink out of."

"Oh, I don't think it does, Mr. Orang-outang," said Tommy Smith, "because they're not spelt——"

"Spilt!" said the orang-outang. "Of course they're not. We can't spill them, because they're fixed in the tree. They're a part of it, you know. We can splash the water out of them, over each other, though, and sometimes that's very good fun."

"Oh, do you ever do that, Mr. Orang-outang?" said Tommy Smith. He saw it was no use explaining.

"Why, how could it be fun if we didn't?" said the orang-outang. "But that's after drinking when we're not thirsty any longer. Then, if there should happen to be two of us, and we're not too old to be frolicsome, to do that is pleasant enough. But, of course, bowls are really made to drink out of, and drinking, when one's thirsty, is a much greater pleasure than splashing. Oh, it's delightful, after a fine feast of fruit, to lie at full length along some great bough and suck up water and feel it gurgling down one's throat."

"Yes, I see what you mean now, Mr. Orang-outang," said Tommy Smith. "I didn't know that was how you drank."

"Of course we've other ways as well," said the orang-outang. "We don't always drink out of bowls. Sometimes we prefer cups or pitchers."

"Cups or pitchers, Mr. Orang-outang?" said Tommy Smith. "Only I know you mean something else really, so I wish you'd tell me."

"Why, you've heard of the pitcher-plant, haven't you?" said the orang-outang.

"Yes, I think I have, Mr. Orang-outang," said Tommy Smith.

"Well, we've got it up there," said the orang-outang.

"Up in the trees, do you mean, Mr. Orang-outang?" said Tommy Smith.

"Of course I do," said the orang-outang. "That's where it grows—on the large branches of the great forest trees that we live amongst. It doesn't really belong to the trees. It isn't their own blossom, but only grows upon them, just as other plants grow on the ground."

"Oh, that's like the mistletoe, Mr. Orang-outang," said Tommy Smith.

"It's like ever so many plants where I live," said the orang-outang. "There are pitchers in our trees, of various shapes and sizes, for us to drink out of, and the largest hold quite enough water to give us a very good sip. Of course, when we've once emptied them we can't fill them again, but that doesn't matter, because there are lots of others all ready filled. Those are our pitchers, and our cups are the flower-cups."

"Oh, but those are not very large, are they, Mr. Orang-outang?" said Tommy Smith.

"That depends on the flower," said the orang-outang, "and, in the forests where I live, there are flowers larger than a man's head."

"Oh, are there really, Mr. Orang-outang?" said Tommy Smith. He had never heard of flowers so large as that.

"One is, anyhow," said the orang-outang. "There are a good many cups of water in a flower-cup like that."

"Does it grow on trees, too, Mr. Orang-outang?" asked Tommy Smith.

"It grows on creepers," the orang-outang answered, "and the creepers are all about amongst the trees. They climb up them, and hang down from them, but this very large flower generally grows on the lower parts of these creepers, where they creep along the ground. So when we orang-outangs want it, we have to come down for it. It is of a deep red colour, like a meat, and smells so pleasantly that all sorts of flies that like meat come and settle on it."

Tommy Smith thought that he would rather see that flower than smell it, but he didn't say so to the orang-outang, because it would not have altered his opinion.

"They must be wonderful forests where you live, Mr. Orang-outang," he said.

"Oh, wonderful," the orang-outang answered. "So much eating and drinking that life is one long pleasure."

"That sounds rather greedy, Mr. Orang-outang," said Tommy Smith.

"It isn't really," said the orang-outang, "because we're hungry all the time we're eating, and thirsty all the time we're drinking."

"I suppose there are a lot of fruits for you to eat there, Mr. Orang-outang," said Tommy Smith.

"Oh, ever so many," said the orang-outang. "There are all the different dates and nuts that grow on ever so many kinds of palm-trees. But every tree has its fruit, and I can't tell you what superior tastes some of them have. Why, the highest of trees seems too low when one's eating a mango, but if it is quite a low one one's eating it in, then it's as if it got higher. That's the effect it has. But I won't talk of it."

"Why not, Mr. Orang-outang?" said Tommy Smith. He thought he would like to hear something more about a fruit like that.

"Because there's another," the orang-outang explained, "that sends one up so much higher when one eats it, that it makes all the rest not worth talking of. It's no use trying to talk of mangos when one's thinking of durians all the while."

"What funny names you have for your fruits, Mr. Orang-outang," said Tommy Smith (and yet the names seemed the least funny part of them). "Mango and durian."

"As for that," said the orang-outang, "they grow in the mango and durian trees, so it would be funny if they had any other name."

"What sort of fruit is the durian, Mr. Orang-outang?" said Tommy Smith.

"I can tell you what it looks like," said the orang-outang. "That's easy. It's about the size and shape of a coconut, only dark green, and covered all over with sharp, thorny spines, so that, until it's ripe, there's no taking hold of it. However, that doesn't matter, because, until it is ripe, one doesn't want to take hold of it."

"And when it is ripe, Mr. Orang-outang?" said Tommy Smith.

"Oh, then the rind bursts," said the orang-outang, "so that one can get one's fingers into it, and pull it open, quite easily. It turns yellow then, too. Well, that's what it looks like. As for what it tastes like and smells like——"

"Smells like?" said Tommy Smith. "Then does it smell as nice as it tastes, Mr. Orang-outang?" But, for some time, the orang-outang made no answer at all, but sat in his heap of straw, with the fingers of his hands bent towards each other, in front of him, and almost touching, as if he were holding something, and a dreamy expression in his eyes, which were half closed and turned upwards. At last he opened his eyes and said: "Excuse me, I thought I was eating one." But, almost directly, he shut them again—or at least nearly—and said, "and smelling——" but in such a low tone that Tommy Smith could only just hear those two words.

"You needn't go to sleep because you think you are, Mr. Orang-outang," said Tommy Smith. "What does it taste like and——"

"Oh, like all sorts of things," said the orang-outang, "like custard and cream and butter and almonds, onions and cheese, potatoes, soup, gravy, and puddings."

"Oh, yes, that's all very well, Mr. Orang-outang," said Tommy Smith—for he thought he was laughing at him. "I don't see how one fruit can taste like all those things."

"Oh, that isn't nearly all," said the orang-outang. "Those are only just a few of the things that can be described, but it tastes like a lot of others, too, that can only be imagined."

"What sort of things, Mr. Orang-outang?" said Tommy Smith.

"Haven't I just said that you've got to imagine them?" said the orang-outang. "Some people can't imagine half of them, and others only get to three-quarters. To imagine them all, one must have a very high forehead indeed."

"I don't see what that can have to do with it, Mr. Orang-outang," said Tommy Smith.

"People with high foreheads," said the orang-outang, putting his hand on his own, "imagine things better than people whose foreheads are not high. The higher the forehead is of a person who's eating a durian, the more things it tastes like, to him."

"It's a very funny fruit indeed, Mr. Orang-outang, if you really mean all that," said Tommy Smith.

"I shouldn't miss it so much if I didn't," said the orang-outang. "You can read it in quite serious books, and no respectable orang-outang would joke upon such a subject. Why, even the tiger delights in it."

"The tiger, Mr. Orang-outang?" cried Tommy Smith, in great surprise. "I thought he only ate meat."

"Meat and durians," said the orang-outang. "You'll find that in serious books too."

"It's very funny, Mr. Orang-outang," said Tommy Smith. "And what does it smell like?"

"Like everything I've told you about, only much stronger, as if they'd all been kept a long time," said the orang-outang. "It smells so strong that some poor, cowardly white people can never come near enough to it to taste it, so you can think what they miss. But others are braver, and when once they have tasted it, then they like smelling it too."

Tommy Smith thought that this must be the most wonderful fruit he had ever heard of, but he was not quite sure whether he would like it himself, and he thought he had better not ask anything more about it, because the orang-outang was beginning to shut his eyes again.

"Then do you always live and eat and drink in the trees, Mr. Orang-outang?" he said, as soon as he noticed this, so as to keep him awake.

"Not quite always," said the orang-outang. "Only

we keep there as much as we can, because we don't like coming down to the ground unless we're obliged to."

"Why not, Mr. Orang-outang?" said Tommy Smith.

"Oh, it's such an uncomfortable way of getting about," said the orang-outang. "No branches or creepers, so that there's only oneself to swing from."

"I don't see how you can swing from yourself, Mr. Orang-outang," said Tommy Smith.

"Why, like this," said the orang-outang, and getting out of his heap of straw, he began to go over the floor of his cage, by putting the knuckles of his hands on the ground, and swinging his body forward between his two arms, just as a man does on crutches. He just made his arms into crutches, and looked very much like a cripple. Tommy Smith saw now that he really had not got a tail, but, of course, he didn't say anything about it, because he had promised not to.

"Oh, that is funny, Mr. Orang-outang," he cried. "But can't you walk upright, like a man?"

"Not like a ground-man," said the orang-outang. "You see, my feet turn in, in the proper way for catching hold of the branches of trees, but not for putting them flat on the ground. I can walk on them sideways, like this, but then I have to use my hands as well. Perhaps I might be taught to walk upright—with a stick, perhaps— but it would only be a trick."

The orang-outang had walked up and down his cage, in his own way, on the knuckles of his hands and the sides of his feet several times before finishing this sentence. His arms were so long that his head and the front part of his body were quite high up, compared to the rest of him, so that he really looked more like a man stooping than a dog or other animal walking. Then he climbed up to the roof of his cage, and went along that much more easily, swinging himself first by one arm and then the other, just to show Tommy Smith how he went about in his forests, though, of course, as there were no trees growing in his cage, he could not show him this very well. "There," he said, as he came back to his straw again, "that is how we orang-outangs have to walk, when we come down from our safe, solid trees on to the uncertain and treacherous ground."

"I should think trees were much more uncertain than the ground, Mr. Orang-outang," said Tommy Smith.

"What, to walk on?" said the orang-outang. "Give me the firm, secure bough."

"But one can fall off the branch of a tree, Mr. Orang-outang," said Tommy Smith.

"On to another," said the orang-outang. "That's just it. In a tree, if one does make a slip, there are branches and creepers all about, to catch hold of, but there's nothing at all between you and the ground, if you happen to slip, when you're on it. As for turning upside down, when you feel yourself going, and hanging from it, head downwards, it's not to be done. Why, you can't even hang from it by your hands."

"Of course you can't, Mr. Orang-outang," said Tommy Smith. "But then you don't want to."

"You mayn't want to, because you're a ground-man," said the orang-outang, "but I should like to very much indeed."

"I don't see what good it would do, Mr. Orang-outang," said Tommy Smith.

"It would do me good, I'm sure," said the orang-outang. "I don't like being on anything I can't hang from. It gives me a giddy feeling. I like to hang from something and look down on something else. But there's no doing that with the ground. It's so large and flat that one can't even get one's arms round it, much less one's fingers or toes—so that one never has a sense of security."

"But I suppose you sleep on it, don't you, Mr. Orang-outang?" said Tommy Smith. Of course he knew that monkeys slept in trees, but they were so much smaller than this big orang-outang he was talking to. He thought such a large animal could only go to sleep safely on the ground.

"Sleep on it!" cried the orang-outang, "I should think not, indeed. I'm not quite so reckless as that. If it's unsafe in the day-time, when the sun's shining, what must it be at night, when it's dark?"

"But aren't you afraid of falling out of the trees when you're asleep, Mr. Orang-outang?" said Tommy Smith.

"I should have to be a very nervous orang-outang if I were," the orang-outang answered. "Why, how often do you fall out of your bed, then?"

"I shouldn't have very far to fall, even if I did," said Tommy Smith.

"But do you often?" said the orang-outang.

"Oh, no, of course not, Mr. Orang-outang," said Tommy Smith, "I don't ever fall out of it."

"I don't either," said the orang-outang, "and when there are two people who never fall out of their beds, it's as safe for the one whose bed is high up as for the one whose bed is low down. Can you see that?"

"Yes, of course I can, Mr. Orang-outang," said Tommy Smith, a little impatiently, for that orang-outang's hand had gone to his forehead again. "But do you make a bed for yourself, in the trees, then?"

"I have to," said the orang-outang. "There are no servants in Treeland. One must do things for oneself there."

"Oh, I didn't mean that," said Tommy Smith. (Of course he had not thought of servants.) "Do tell me how you make it, Mr. Orang-outang."

"Why, I pull off some nice leafy branches," said the orang-outang, "and lay them across the growing branches of the tree I am in, so as to make a nice, dry, soft mattress to lie on. It doesn't matter how dark it gets then, for I feel leaves and branches all about me, and I know that there are ever so many more, and a lot of strong, reliable creepers, as well, between me and the ground. Then, you know, a tree sways—almost always just a little, and sometimes, oh, quite famously—so, of course, my bed sways with it, and to sway in one's bed gives one a safe, settled feeling that helps to send one to sleep. Oh, I do like swaying in bed, so. The stars peep at me through the leaves, as I go up and down, and the moon drops silver upon me. It may be meant for the fairies, but I get some of it too."

"The fairies, Mr. Orang-outang?" cried Tommy Smith, for he felt quite excited.

"Yes, they come to the flowers in the moonlight," said the orang-outang, "and when there are any near my bed, especially the large white ones that open at night, and that they're so fond of, I can watch them as they hover, for a little, in front of them, and then dart away and come back and hover again. Their wings are only like a film round them then, they move so quickly, but their bodies don't move at all, and you can see them uncurl those long thin tubes of theirs that they suck up the nectar with, and fit them into the tubes of the flowers. It's like a thread tying them and the flower together, and the moonlight makes it a silver one. I've often wondered how they can stay so still and move so quickly, at the same time."

"I believe it's the moths that you mean, Mr. Orang-outang," said Tommy Smith. "They're not fairies."

"That's what we call them in Treeland," said the orang-outang. "They're the night-fairies. The day-fairies are much brighter, because they get their colours from the sun, and the night-fairies get them from the moon."

"They're only moths and butterflies," said Tommy Smith. He felt quite disappointed.

182

"Have it your own way," said the orang-outang, "but they're fairies in Treeland, and they come round my bed, every night. That's why I like the night ones best. They bring me dreams, I believe, and the wind and the rustling leaves sing lullabies to me. Is your bed like that? Oh, I'm well cared for—very well cared for in Treeland."

"But the wind comes everywhere, you know, Mr. Orang-outang," said Tommy Smith, "and so you could sleep on the ground, in the moonlight, too."

"Oh, the moonlight's not nearly so pure there," the orang-outang answered. "It should be strained through the leaves—filtered moonlight's the purest. Besides, it would be too much silver dropped upon me, unless I were under a tree, and who would sleep under a tree when he might sleep in one? No orang-outang would. Trees don't rock one then, and the ground doesn't ever— not properly. It only rocks when there's an earthquake, and then it rocks too much. It would be dreadful to have to go to sleep without any swaying at all, and then to wake up in an earthquake."

"But an earthquake wouldn't be nice in a tree either, Mr. Orang-outang," said Tommy Smith.

"It wouldn't be nearly so nasty," said the orang-outang, "and at least there'd be something to catch hold of. No, no, the ground's all very well for ground-men, they're so venturesome. But I like safety, so I keep away from dangerous places."

"Isn't it because you climb so well that you never come out of the trees, Mr. Orang-outang?" said Tommy Smith.

"We call it walking in Treeland," said the orang-outang. "I can walk properly there, but there's another reason, and a still stronger one, why I don't come down if I can help it."

"What is it, please, Mr. Orang-outang?" asked Tommy Smith.

"It's because I'm afraid of becoming a low-down ground-man instead of a high-up tree-man," the orang-outang answered.

Tommy Smith thought it best to try not to be angry, because it wouldn't do any good, and might stop the conversation. So he only said (though it was in rather a cold sort of way): "I don't see how you can become one, as you're not one, Mr. Orang-outang."

"Much more easily than if I were one," said the orang-outang. "You can't become what you are, you know."

"If it comes to that, Mr. Orang-outang," said Tommy Smith, "you can't always become what you're not, either." He didn't want to be put down by an orang-outang.

"But you can sometimes," said the orang-outang. "And I have a theory. Do you know what a theory is?"

"Isn't it something that one thinks oneself, but nobody else does?" said Tommy Smith—for those were the kind of ones his father had.

"That doesn't so much matter," said the orang-outang. "Having it's the great thing, and to have it, one must have a high forehead. I have, as you see, and my theory is that ground-men used to be tree-men, like myself, only they came down from their trees on to the ground, which made them ground-men. That's simple. A child could see that part of it. And then the longer they stayed on the ground, after they had come down, the more they were ground-men—which is simple, too—till at last they weren't orang-outangs any longer. How could they be? Well, that's my theory."

"It's a very funny one, Mr. Orang-outang," said Tommy Smith. "Why are there orang-outangs still, if they all changed——?"

"Not all," said the orang-outang. "There were some who saw what was happening to them and they got back to their trees, and that saved them. That's what we do now. We only stay a very little while when we go down, and then the effect wears off."

"I'm sure it isn't true, Mr. Orang-outang," said Tommy Smith. "How *could* orang-outangs change into men?"

"Gound-men, if you please," said the orang-outang. "We were men to begin with—tree-men. So it wasn't so difficult. It's easy to go down-hill, you know, and going down-tree is just the same. Well, that's my theory."

"Well, I don't believe it, Mr. Orang-outang," said Tommy Smith. "I don't see how you *could* change like that."

"You see, it was gradual," said the orang-outang.

"I think it's all nonsense, Mr. Orang-outang," said Tommy Smith.

"It can't be, because I can prove it," said the orang-outang. "You can't prove nonsense, of course."

"I don't see how you can prove it, Mr. Orang-outang," said Tommy Smith.

"You will, in a minute," said the orang-outang. "You see, if tree-men gradually changed into ground-men they must have been half ground-men before they were quite ground-men, and if some of them had stopped like that then they'd be like that now, and that would prove it. Well, in my country, there are some people who live on the ground in the day-time and sleep in trees at night, so they're half tree-men and half ground-men."

"Are there really, Mr. Orang-outang?" said Tommy Smith. Of course he was very much surprised.

"There really are," said the orang-outang, "and they're only half as wicked as real ground-men. That proves it still more."

"No, it doesn't, Mr. Orang-outang," said Tommy Smith, "because, if it comes to that, why are ground-men, as you call them, so wicked?"

"I think it's something *in* the ground," said the orang-outang.

"*In* the ground, Mr. Orang-outang?" said Tommy Smith.

"I won't be sure," said the orang-outang, "but, at any rate, it keeps on growing."

"Oh, yes, it's all very well, Mr. Orang-outang," said Tommy Smith. "But are you sure men *are* so wicked?"

"Ground-men—oh, quite," said the orang-outang. "Now we come to facts, and in my country they're all of them murderers."

"Oh, no, Mr. Orang-outang, not all of them," said Tommy Smith.

"All of them who can be," said the orang-outang. "There isn't a single one who has either a gun or a blow-pipe, whether he's a Dyak, a Malay, or a White Man, who won't shoot an orang-outang with it, as soon as he sees one. Isn't that awful? Now I ask you."

"Yes, it is, Mr. Orang-outang," said Tommy Smith. And it was what he really thought.

"Although he knows that we're men," the orang-outang went on, "because that's his own name for us. Now, as we are men, of course there are women and children amongst us. But that makes no difference to a ground-man. He shoots them, too, and often both of them together—mothers, I mean, with their little ones hanging round their necks. Isn't it shocking?"

"Yes, Mr. Orang-outang," said Tommy Smith, "I think it's dreadful." He didn't feel at all comfortable, for the orang-outang was looking at him very earnestly, and although, of course, there were differences, yet he looked so like a man, that really it was not pleasant to meet his eye whilst he was talking in that way. In fact, it was so very unpleasant that he had to look down, but that was not good at all, because then he found himself looking at the orang-outang's hands, which was worse, for they looked even more like a man's hands than his face looked like a man's face. They were coarse hands, it is true, but then Tommy Smith knew very well that a great many men have coarse hands too. He had even shaken hands with some who had. So he looked up again. He had felt sure that the orang-outang still had his eyes fixed upon him, and so he had.

"I hope you *really* think it's murder," said the orang-outang, with a very searching look.

"Yes, I do really, Mr. Orang-outang," said Tommy Smith. And he couldn't help hoping that he should never have to meet or speak to a man, when he was grown up, who had shot orang-outangs, especially female orang-outangs with little ones clinging round their necks.

"Why do they kill you, Mr. Orang-outang?" he asked, after a little.

"That's just what I've never been able to understand," said the orang-outang, "because, alive, I am very interesting. I mean that I have very interesting habits, if only people would study them. And yet, of all the ground-men I ever met, either the yellow ones who live in my country, or the white ones who come out to it, not one has ever tried to study my habits. All he did was to shoot me, and then, of course, I hadn't any. One can't have habits after one's dead. Just murder—that's always the ground-man's idea. In fact, he's so fond of it that when he can't find orang-outangs, he murders his own fellow ground-men and women."

"Oh, no, surely, Mr. Orang-outang," said Tommy Smith. "I don't think he can do that."

"Why, of course he can," said the orang-outang, "quite easily. It's the two together that he can't do, and that's the only reason why he doesn't."

Perhaps the men where you live are *very* wicked, Mr. Orang-outang," said Tommy Smith.

"Oh, dreadfully," said the orang-outang. "Why, there are some of the—the Dyaks—who actually set out on expeditions to kill people, and then steal their heads when they're dead."

"Steal their heads, Mr. Orang-outang!" cried Tommy Smith, for he could hardly believe it.

"Indeed they do," said the orang-outang, "though they're the last things that *I* should ever think of stealing. And then sometimes one of them will take a long crooked sort of sword that he always has at his side, out of its sheath, and begin to run about with it. And the first man he meets, he runs that sword through him, and then the next and the next—as many as he does meet—he goes on murdering them all."

"Oh, how dreadful, Mr. Orang-outang," said Tommy Smith. "But does he meet many?"

"As many as he can," the orang-outang answered. "He always goes where there are a lot of other ground-men, and he never stops killing them till one of them has killed him."

"They do seem dreadful men where you live, Mr. Orang-outang," said Tommy Smith.

"Ground-men—yes, they are," said the orang-outang. "What with stealing heads and running about

189

and stabbing with swords, the killing that goes on in my country is something one could hardly believe, even amongst savages. Why, it must come to hundreds in one year."

"Just fancy, Mr. Orang-outang!" said Tommy Smith.

"I really don't know where it will end," said the orang-outang, "and the reason of it all is, that there were some of us orang-outangs who came down from our trees and didn't go back to them again."

"Yes, I know you think that, Mr. Orang-outang," said Tommy Smith.

"I know it by what happens when I come down myself," said the orang-outang.

"But I thought you didn't come down, Mr. Orang-outang," said Tommy Smith.

"We don't as long as we can help it," said the orang-outang. "But sometimes we can't help it, and then, as soon as we get on to the ground, we're wicked directly. We were always quite innocent before."

"Oh, but how are you wicked, Mr. Orang-outang?" asked Tommy Smith. He didn't understand that at all.

"Because we're beginning to be ground-men," said the orang-outang. "That's how it happens."

"But what do you do to make you wicked, Mr. Orang-outang?" asked Tommy Smith.

"Steal," said the orang-outang, in a low voice, and looking down, just as Tommy Smith had done before.

"What, just because you're on the ground, Mr. Orang-outang?" said Tommy Smith.

"If we stayed longer it would get to murder, soon, I dare say," said the orang-outang. "But, of course, we don't want it to, so we go back to our trees as quickly as ever we can."

"Oh, I do wish you'd explain it, Mr. Orang-outang," said Tommy Smith.

"Well, I'll try to, only it's difficult," said the orang-outang. "There we are, one moment, eating our beautiful fruit and things that grow wild in the forest, and not doing any harm at all. It's all happiness and innocence, but, all at once, we see a fine field of ripe rice underneath us, and as soon as we come down to eat it—because, of course, we have to—with the very first mouthful—which is *so* delicious—why, we're stealing."

"It must belong to somebody else, if you are, then, Mr. Orang-outang," said Tommy Smith.

"Of course it does," said the orang-outang, "and as long as we stayed in our trees we never used to steal it, because we were good then. But once out of them, and on the ground, we began not to be good, and then we stole the rice."

"Oh, yes, that's all very well, Mr. Orang-outang," said Tommy Smith, "but you came down when you saw the rice, because you wanted to steal it."

"We wanted to eat it," said the orang-outang—"that was all. Eating was always quite innocent in Treeland, but, on the ground, it got wicked, and turned into stealing, because then we began to be ground-men. That's my theory."

"It's a very funny one, I think, Mr. Orang-outang," said Tommy Smith, for the second time.

"Ingenious is the right word," said the orang-outang, "but the meaning's the same."

"I don't think it's true, Mr. Orang-outang," said Tommy Smith.

"I wish it were not," said the orang-outang.

"Oh, but why, Mr. Orang-outang," said Tommy Smith. He was very surprised to hear him say that, for it didn't sound natural.

"Because if it's true," said the orang-outang, with a very melancholy look, "I shall be a ground-man myself, before long. There are no trees here for me to get back to, for they haven't given me any—not even a single one. I don't call that thing there a tree. Once I got out, and was up one in a moment. Oh, you can't think how good I felt, but they took me out of it, and put me in here again, just to make me as wicked as themselves."

"Oh, but did you really get out, and go up a tree, once, Mr. Orang-outang?" said Tommy Smith.

"Yes, indeed I did," said the orang-outang. "Oh, if only they'd left me in my tree. It was a bad one, it's true—oh, a very bad tree, the poorest I've ever been in. But still it was one, and I made a bed in it. It's there now, the keeper tells me."

"Oh, I would like to see it, Mr. Orang-outang," said Tommy Smith.

"Turn to the right when you go out at this door," said the orang-outang, "and it's the first tree on your right hand."

Tommy Smith was going to say good-bye, because it was getting late and he wanted to see the tree with the orang-outang's bed in it, before he went. But the orang-outang looked at him as if he was asking him to stay just a minute, and then he said:

"Then you don't think it's true, really? It would be dreadful if I did turn into a ground-man, and I have felt so like one lately. Such a bad, bad feeling! It's been worrying me very much, but, of course, if my theory is not true, I shan't. Do you really think it isn't?"

"I'm sure it isn't, Mr. Orang-outang," said Tommy Smith, very decidedly.

"Thank you, thank you ever so much," said the orang-outang. "And now, good-night, because the sun must be setting, and we two always go to bed at the same time."

And then, all at once—almost as soon as he had said this—there was no orang-outang to talk to, any more, only a heap of straw, for he had taken it all up in his arms and thrown it all over himself. It was quite true about the sun setting, and Tommy Smith could only stay just a minute or two, to look at the tree with the bed in it—for that was true too—and then he began to walk home, to tea, as fast as he could. He had really stayed longer than he ought to have done, but then he had a very good excuse for it. And, on his way home, Tommy Smith kept thinking what an interesting animal the orang-outang was, and he couldn't help wondering, sometimes, whether he had not been making fun of him, a little. Of course, if he had, then, perhaps, he was not quite so conceited as he had seemed to be.

www.ingramcontent.com/pod-product-compliance
Lightning Source LLC
Chambersburg PA
CBHW031839090426
42741CB00005B/295